THE POCKET IDIOT'S GUIDE™ TO

Reverse Mortgages

by Jennifer A. Pokorny

ALPHA

A member of Penguin Group (USA) Inc.

To my parents, Bud and Pat Hyland, who told me I could do anything,
and then showed me how every day.

ALPHA BOOKS

Published by the Penguin Group

Penguin Group (USA) Inc., 375 Hudson Street, New York, New York 10014, U.S.A.

Penguin Group (Canada), 10 Alcorn Avenue, Toronto, Ontario, Canada M4V 3B2 (a division of Pearson Penguin Canada Inc.)

Penguin Books Ltd, 80 Strand, London WC2R 0RL, England

Penguin Ireland, 25 St Stephen's Green, Dublin 2, Ireland (a division of Penguin Books Ltd)

Penguin Group (Australia), 250 Camberwell Road, Camberwell, Victoria 3124, Australia (a division of Pearson Australia Group Pty Ltd)

Penguin Books India Pvt Ltd, 11 Community Centre, Panchsheel Park, New Delhi—110 017, India

Penguin Group (NZ), cnr Airborne and Rosedale Roads, Albany, Auckland 1310, New Zealand (a division of Pearson New Zealand Ltd)

Penguin Books (South Africa) (Pty) Ltd, 24 Sturdee Avenue, Rosebank, Johannesburg 2196, South Africa

Penguin Books Ltd, Registered Offices: 80 Strand, London WC2R 0RL, England

Copyright © 2005 by Penguin Group (USA) Inc.

International Standard Book Number: 1-59257-377-0
Library of Congress Catalog Card Number: 2005926959

07 06 05   8 7 6 5 4 3 2 1

Interpretation of the printing code: The rightmost number of the first series of numbers is the year of the book's printing; the rightmost number of the second series of numbers is the number of the book's printing. For example, a printing code of 05-1 shows that the first printing occurred in 2005.

Printed in the United States of America

Note: This publication contains the opinions and ideas of its author. It is intended to provide helpful and informative material on the subject matter covered. It is sold with the understanding that the author and publisher are not engaged in rendering professional services in the book. If the reader requires personal assistance or advice, a competent professional should be consulted.

The author and publisher specifically disclaim any responsibility for any liability, loss, or risk, personal or otherwise, which is incurred as a consequence, directly or indirectly, of the use and application of any of the contents of this book.

Most Alpha books are available at special quantity discounts for bulk purchases for sales promotions, premiums, fund-raising, or educational use. Special books, or book excerpts, can also be created to fit specific needs.

For details, write: Special Markets, Alpha Books, 375 Hudson Street, New York, NY 10014.

Contents

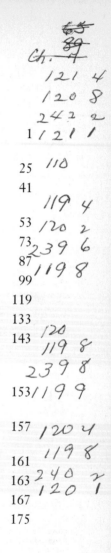

Introduction

We think of retirement as the "golden years," when we finally have both the time and money to do all the things we've always wanted to do. Travel the world. Pursue a hobby. Volunteer at the school. Or spend more time with family.

Today's retirees are living longer and healthier, thanks to improvements in lifestyle, diet, and health care. And the number of retirees continues to increase as a percentage of the population. In fact, as the baby boomers begin to retire, one in five Americans will be "seniors."

The Social Security system is strained, and the Pension Benefit Guarantee system is warning that it may not be able to cover all pensions fully if company defaults continue. The full retirement age has been pushed back by five years, from 62 to 67. Changes in Social Security benefits are inevitable.

Planning for your retirement has never been more important. Whether you are looking forward to retirement, currently retired, or trying to help a parent, the reverse mortgage is an option that you should be aware of.

A reverse mortgage can be used effectively to provide additional income to current retirees, as cash to make modifications so you can continue to live in your home, or as a financial planning tool for estate planning. It is a versatile program with many options.

However, it is not the right choice for every situation. It is a very expensive loan if used to provide money for a short period of time, and sometimes it just doesn't provide enough money to do what you need. In that case, taking a reverse mortgage would be like throwing out the baby with the bathtub, a really bad idea. Sometimes, the smart choice is to sell your house and move, even though it is not what you want to do. Picking the wrong mortgage can also cost you money, as you will see from examples in the book. The purpose of this book is to explain what reverse mortgages are, and how they really work. Chapter 1 provides background information and discusses the concepts behind the reverse mortgages. Chapter 2 walks you through some options to reverse mortgages and gives you some tools to help you make an informed choice. Chapter 3 explores single-purpose mortgages, which might provide an alternative to reverse mortgages.

Chapters 4 through 6 introduce the three major reverse mortgage programs currently available: the Home Equity Conversion Mortgage (HECM), the Home Keeper, and the Cash Account. The chapters review the specific program requirements for each loan, how the loans work and how payments are calculated, and give specific examples of when you might choose one loan over the other.

Chapters 7 and 8 walk you through the application process, counseling, and the approval process. Chapter 9 provides a detailed discussion of the appraisal, how house values are determined, and steps you can take to increase the value of your home. In Chapter 10, we take a look at what happens after all the papers are signed and the loan has been finalized.

As a loan officer, I know that theory and practice are not the same. So I have tried to include information about the real world, drawing information from loans that I have done and the experiences of other loan officers in the field.

Throughout the book you will find the following sidebars, which explain terms, provide tips and money-saving ideas, and warn about potential pitfalls.

Talk the Talk

These provide definitions of terms and concepts that you might not be familiar with.

Good Cents

Here you'll find useful tips and information as well as money-saving ideas and suggestions.

CAUTION

Use Caution

These sidebars alert you to the possible pitfalls associated with reverse mortgages, and suggest ways you can avoid being tripped up.

Acknowledgments

I would like to thank my "boss," Larry Bullock, for sharing many of his own experiences with me; Peter Bell, president of the National Reverse Mortgage Lenders Association, for his continuing support of the industry; and all the people at Financial Freedom for their assistance, but particularly those in Lender Support.

I also want to thank Kim Lionetti for tracking me down, Tom Stevens for putting up with me, and both Ginny Bess and Jennifer Connolly who edited this book. It is a better book because of their efforts.

Special Thanks to the Technical Reviewer

The Pocket Idiot's Guide to Reverse Mortgages was reviewed by an expert who double-checked the accuracy of what you'll learn here, to help us ensure that this book gives you everything you need to know about reverse mortgages. Special thanks are extended to Peter Bell, President, National Reverse Mortgage Lenders Association.

Trademarks

All terms mentioned in this book that are known to be or are suspected of being trademarks or service marks have been appropriately capitalized. Alpha Books and Penguin Group (USA) Inc. cannot attest to the accuracy of this information. Use of a term in this book should not be regarded as affecting the validity of any trademark or service mark.

What Is a Reverse Mortgage?

In This Chapter

- What a reverse mortgage is and reasons for obtaining one
- Benefits and drawbacks of reverse mortgages
- Eligibility requirements for reverse mortgages

In this chapter, we cover some of the background: how reverse mortgages evolved, how they work, and what their benefits and drawbacks are. Basic definitions are introduced here, and covered in more detail in later chapters. Common questions about reverse mortgages in general are covered at the end of the chapter.

Forward Mortgages

Now let's take a short step back in time. What we call conventional or forward mortgages have their roots in the Depression era of the 1930s. In fact, most of our banking practices were established during that period, in part to ensure that a repeat of the Stock Market Crash of 1929, and the depression that followed, never happen again.

When Franklin D. Roosevelt took office in 1933, the country was in the depths of the Great Depression. During his first 100 days in office, he implemented a number of programs designed to provide relief to out-of-work citizens, create jobs, and stimulate the economy. Collectively, these programs were called the New Deal for Americans. These included *Social Security*, the Federal Housing Administration (FHA) and Fannie Mae (FNMA).

Talk the Talk

The **Social Security** Act of 1935 is perhaps the best known of the New Deal programs. It provides pensions for workers, unemployment insurance, and aid for widows, orphans, and disabled persons. The retirement age at that time was 65 years old.

When Roosevelt took office, only one in ten American families owned a home. Over 2 million construction workers were out of jobs. And loans of that period were for approximately 50 percent of the house value, and had to be repaid within 3 to 5 years. The FHA changed the ways loans were made.

The FHA does not actually make loans. Instead, the agency insures banks and lenders against losses as long as the loans meet the FHA's criteria. And because lenders are guaranteed that they will not lose money, the lenders are willing to loan a higher percentage of a house's value.

The FHA developed an 80 percent loan-to-value loan program, which required the borrower to put down only 20 percent of the house cost. It also established a nationwide qualification system based on a person's ability to repay the loan, and it lengthened the loan period to 15 years. The 15-year loan eventually evolved into the standard 30-year loan we are familiar with today.

The second big change to the industry was the creation of Fannie Mae in 1938. Their mission was to increase the amount of money available for home mortgages, so more people would have the opportunity to buy homes. FNMA did this by developing a secondary market in which to sell loans. FNMA also developed a set of criteria and lending policies, which the lenders had to adhere to. These differ somewhat from the FHA's policies, but we'll discuss that in more detail in Chapters 4 and 5.

Like the FHA, FNMA does not actually lend money. FNMA reviews and buys loans and resells them to investors, ensuring a constant flow of mortgage money. This has the effect of making more money available for more people to buy houses.

A mortgage is simply a loan that is "secured" by real estate. When you buy a house, the deed is in your name, and the lender records a "mortgage note" that describes the details of the loan, such as how long the loan term is and how it will be repaid. The deed and mortgage note are recorded at the courthouse.

To obtain a loan, you typically must pay a small amount toward the purchase price (the down payment), and take out a mortgage to pay the balance of the cost of the home. A portion of the mortgage payment each month is applied toward the principal (the purchase price), and a larger portion of the money is applied toward the interest due on the loan. This is a conventional, or forward, mortgage. You borrow money, and pay a small amount each month until the loan has been repaid.

Each month, you also gain a little more *equity*— which is the difference between what the house is worth and what you owe on the mortgage. Eventually, the loan is repaid and the mortgage note is "released." When you pay off the loan, you own 100 percent equity in your home.

> ### $ Talk the Talk
>
> **Equity** is the difference between what the house is worth and what you owe for a mortgage or any other loan, judgment, or lien. Equity grows as you pay off existing debt, and as the value of real estate increases.

Reverse Mortgages

Just as its name implies, a reverse mortgage works in the opposite manner of a forward mortgage. A reverse mortgage allows older homeowners, those over the age of 62, to tap into the equity in their homes to generate additional income—without having to sell the house to get it. Instead of making payments, the homeowner receives a lump sum or monthly payments for as long as he or she lives in the home.

Interest is charged against the loan amount, but the homeowner is not required to repay the loan as long as he lives in the home. The loan and accrued interest is repaid when the homeowner dies or sells the home.

The first reverse mortgages were made in the United States in the early '60s by individual banks and insurance companies. Some local governments joined in and offered *single-purpose reverse mortgages* for health care or for repairs. Like early loan programs, the requirements and terms varied by location.

Talk the Talk

Single-purpose reverse mortgages were generally available for low- or very low-income homeowners only. These were for very specific purposes, such as weather-proofing or to pay health-care costs for homeowners over 62, who were not qualified under other programs. The payments on loans were limited to a specific dollar amount (for example, not to exceed $20,000), or a specific time period (5 to 10 years). When limits had been reached, no more money was available. The benefit was that the loan did not have to be repaid until the homeowner died, moved out, or sold the home.

In many cases, there were no guarantees that the homeowner would not "outlive" the reverse mortgage loan or that the heirs would not be liable if the value of the loan grew to more than the house value. Thus, early reverse mortgages were considered risky.

In the late 1980s, the FHA launched a trial program for reverse mortgages, known as the Home Equity Conversion Mortgage (HECM), and Fannie Mae announced that it would buy these FHA-insured mortgages. The first year, 157 HECM loans were made. In 1996, Fannie Mae launched its own version of the reverse mortgage, known as the Home Keeper.

As with early conventional loans, the government-insured program changed the way the industry worked. The government-insured loans are "non-recourse" loans. With a non-recourse loan, only the value of the house can be used to repay the loan, so heirs will not owe additional money if the homeowner lives beyond their expected lifespan.

The FHA insures lenders against losses if house values decline or homeowners live unexpectedly long. The result is that the FHA loan often gives homeowners a higher payout than other loans, making it the most popular choice for most borrowers.

Good Cents

Reverse mortgages are not just a U.S. phenomenon. In the United Kingdom, the Safe Home Income Plan (SHIP) was established in 1991. Canada's plan is known as CHIP, the Canadian Home Income Plan. Australia, Singapore, and Hong Kong are beginning to offer some form of reverse mortgage.

The French government supports a private form of reverse mortgage, dating from the Middle Ages, known as *viager*. A buyer puts a small down payment on a home, and pays the homeowner monthly payments *en viager* (for life). When the seller dies, the buyer gets the title to the house.

Benefits of Reverse Mortgages

The reverse mortgage provides an opportunity for older homeowners to tap the equity in their homes. Money can be used for any purpose, and the flexible payment plans allow it to be tailored to fit many different needs. There are no income and few credit requirements, so people with less-than-perfect credit generally qualify for the loan.

Stay in Home

Many senior homeowners have owned their homes for many years, and would like to remain in their current homes. Their friends and support network (church, doctors, and social groups) are nearby, and their homes hold memories of their lives. Often, they don't want to move. It's scary, emotionally draining, and physically exhausting, no matter what the age. And they don't want to give up their independence.

Equity is like a savings account, and the reverse mortgage is one key you can use to tap it. The reverse mortgage was designed to give senior homeowners access to this equity, so they can continue to live in their homes as long as they choose.

The funds can be used as additional income, to make needed repairs or modifications to the home, for medical care, or even to hire occasional help to assist with heavy chores.

Repayments

No repayment of the loan is required as long as you live in your home and meet the terms of the loan. In general, the terms are that you agree to keep the home in good repair and you continue to pay the taxes and the homeowner's insurance on the property, which are things you would do anyway.

When you die or leave your home for good, such as move to a nursing home, move in with the kids, or hit the lottery and move to Florida, the loan becomes due. The home may be sold, and any remaining equity is yours or the heirs'. If the heirs wish to keep the home, they may take out a conventional mortgage to repay the loan.

Non-Recourse

The reverse mortgage is a "non-recourse" loan. This means that only the value of the home may be used to repay the loan. So if the real estate values in the area of your home drop for some reason (depression, change of area use, or even just a shift in population), you or your heirs will owe only the value of the house when it is sold.

For example, let's assume the house is worth $150,000 when Aunt Rita takes out the reverse mortgage at age 62. She chooses to finance the closing costs and receive a lump sum of $79,800. When she dies 26 years later, the loan has grown to $158,000. But the plant that was the major employer in town has moved and no one wants to buy houses in town anymore. So the house is finally sold for $149,000. Then $149,000 is owed on the loan. No other balance is due.

If the house sold for $175,000, then $158,000 would be repaid for the loan, and the remaining $17,000 in equity would belong to the heirs.

If your family members wish to keep the home, you/they can take out a regular mortgage to pay off the reverse mortgage, or pay off the reverse mortgage with proceeds of life insurance (if there is a policy) or by some other means. The choice is up to them.

Minimal Qualifications

Requirements for private reverse mortgages may vary, but most programs require that a homeowner be 62 years or older, own their own home, or have a mortgage small enough to be paid off by the reverse mortgage. A reverse mortgage can only be made on the homeowner's primary residence. In addition, the home must meet certain minimum property standards set by FHA or FNMA.

Most home types qualify for some type of reverse mortgage. Your home must be in good repair. If repairs are needed, they can often be handled through the reverse mortgage process. (This is discussed in detail in Chapters 7 and 9.)

There is no income requirement for a reverse mortgage because there is no expectation that the homeowner will repay the loan while living in the home.

There are also minimal credit requirements. These include …

- The homeowner is not currently in bank-ruptcy.
- There are no current liens against the property.
- The homeowner is not delinquent on any federal debt.

If one of these requirements is not met, the problem has to be addressed. Often the problem can be resolved by using the reverse mortgage to pay off the debt. Consumer debt, like credit cards, is not considered and does not have to be paid in order to get a reverse loan.

Mortgage Proceeds

There are a number of payment options with the reverse mortgage, and the FHA-insured loan offers the greatest flexibility of payment plans. You can receive a lump sum of the entire loan balance, you can establish a credit line and use the money when you need it, or you can receive a monthly payment to supplement your income. Or you can combine these, taking some money at *closing* and having a portion paid in monthly installments.

 Talk the Talk

Closing is when the final documents are signed and the loan is complete. Three copies of original documents are often required, versus one to two copies for a standard closing. So there are a lot of documents to sign. There is a three-day waiting period, called the three-day right of recission, during which you can change your mind. On the fourth day, funding, the money for the loan, becomes available.

Drawbacks

Many of the pitfalls of early reverse mortgages have been eliminated, but there are some disadvantages to the reverse mortgages which you should be aware of.

Cost

The single biggest objection block for most people is the cost of the reverse mortgage, which is typically 5 percent for an FHA-insured mortgage. If the house's value is under $100,000, the percentage of the costs may be even higher.

The costs for the FHA-insured mortgage include a 2 percent mortgage insurance premium, a 2 percent origination fee (or $2,000, whichever is higher), and standard closing costs. The closing costs include the property appraisal, title insurance, and government recording fees for your mortgage.

In addition, lenders charge a monthly servicing fee (generally $25–$35/monthy) to keep track of the loan. FHA-insured loans also pay a monthly mortgage insurance premium of .5 percent a month.

It's a lot of money, but let's ask "Compared to what?" A conventional loan? This is not a conventional loan and trying to compare it to one is like comparing apples to pineapples.

If you take out a regular or conventional FHA-insured loan, you will pay a 1.5 percent up-front premium for mortgage insurance. The reverse mortgage is 2 percent.

A conventional FHA-insured loan will charge a monthly fee of .5 of a percent mortgage insurance for condominiums, and a rate based on the amount you borrow for all other loans. The monthly charge for the reverse mortgage is ½ of a percent. So you would pay the same monthly fee for mortgage insurance on a conventional FHA loan and a reverse mortgage.

With a conventional loan, you often pay points (a percentage of the loan amount) for the lowest rate, or a yield spread premium (money paid by the lender to the loan officer, correspondent lender, or broker) to make the loan. Either way, you are paying an origination fee of some sort to get the loan. But it is often built into the loan costs, and you do not see it as money "out-of-pocket" so it doesn't hurt as much.

Servicing fees are paid to the lender on conventional loans as well. For a reverse mortgage, servicing fees are $25-$35 a month. With a conventional loan, the servicing fee is based on a percentage of the loan. This is negotiated between the loan seller (bank) and the servicing company, but might be as high as .25 of a percent of the loan payment each month. But again, these costs are built into the loan and are reflected in a higher interest rate, so you don't see them.

Red Tape

Government-insured loans are time-consuming and more complicated than conventional loans.

Most reverse mortgages are government-insured. The paperwork can be daunting, and is often confusing because of the number of required *disclosures* covering everything from rates to privacy.

$ **Talk the Talk**

Disclosures are written statements explaining various policies and your rights under the law. In addition to Federal government regulations, each state has its own set of laws and guidelines, so you might have disclosures from both the federal and state governments covering the same items. Disclosures cover everything from your right to privacy, right to receive a copy of the appraisal, and how rates might be calculated, to how your credit score is arrived at.

The lender has forms, the title company has forms, and the government requires yet a different set of forms. You will sign 25 or more pages to apply for the loan, and as much as four times that many documents at closing.

Efforts are constantly being made to simplify the paperwork and make disclosures easier to understand, but obtaining a reverse mortgage will probably never be a simple process.

Variable Rates

Most reverse mortgages are Adjustable Rate Mortgages, commonly known as ARMs. The loans are based on an *index*, which is a "cost of funds" measurement such as the 1-year Treasury bill (T-bill) rate, or the 1-month Certificate of Deposit (CD) rate. A "margin" or fixed percentage rate is added to the index to determine the current interest rate charged. Following is the equation for determining the interest rate:

Index + Margin = Interest Rate

Talk the Talk

An **index** is a published measure you can find in the financial section of most newspapers. For our purposes, an index is what it costs to borrow money. There are a number of well-known indexes. The 1-year Treasury bill rate is the percentage rate that a 1-year Treasury bond would pay if you bought one today. The 1-month CD rate is the rate you would be paid if you put your money into a 1-month CD.

Like most ARMs, the reverse mortgage has a "cap," the maximum interest rate that can be charged on the loan. The cap can be as little as 5 percent or as high as 16 percent.

Reverse mortgages are risky, but not for you. They are a calculated risk for the lender. There is no way to know how long you will live, so the lender can only guess how long you might keep the loan. It might be 5 years—or it might be 50.

The house is security for the loan. You can probably guess whether housing values in your area are going to go up or down over the next year or two, but how about over the next 25 years? You can make a prediction based on past experience, but stuff happens—wars, natural disasters, changes in employment, changes in the economy, school systems, crime rates. Changes, both gradual and sudden, influence house values.

Remember that the house is the only security that the lender has for this loan. So if the house value decreases, the lender (or government) will lose money.

And interest rates? Are they going to go up or down? How much and for how long? If the lender is charging you 5 percent, but current interest rates are 11 percent, they are losing money. On the other hand, if they charge you 11 percent and current interest rates are 5 percent, then they are making a big profit and you are paying a very high rate for your loan. Either way, there is a risk involved.

An ARM shares the risk between the borrower and the lender. If interest rates go up, then the lender is still earning a fair rate for the loan. If they go down, then the homeowner gets the benefit of the lower rate.

Insufficient Funds

The reverse mortgage is not a conventional loan, and you will not be able to borrow 100 percent of the value of your home. The amount of money you can receive will be influenced by several factors: the current interest rate, your age, the value of your home, or the limit imposed by the loan itself.

This makes it difficult to estimate what you can borrow. A rule of thumb is roughly half the house value if you are 62, minus the closing costs and service fee set aside. At age 82, you may receive 75 to 80 percent of the value of the home. Loan limits can change this dramatically.

For example, if you live in a $300,000 home, but the area limit is $160,000, then the loan will be calculated on the lower amount. So you could receive about half of the geographic limit, or $80,000, rather than the $150,000 you might expect.

You might ask why you can't borrow the full value of the house. Put yourself in the lender's shoes for just a minute. You are lending someone money, but have no idea when it will be paid back. They are promising to pay it back from the house when they sell it, but you have no idea what the house may be worth at that time. Would you tie all your money up with that kind of bet?

Probably not. You would want to be sure there is enough money left from the sale of the house to pay you back, and to pay a reasonable rate of interest on that money while you wait. After all, you would be earning interest if the money was in the bank, in a CD, or invested in the stock market (well, we hope so anyway).

Using historic averages, house values may grow 4 percent a year, and let's suppose the average interest rate over the life of the loan will be about 6 percent. Then you have to calculate average lifespan—so guess that the average borrower may live to be age 100. Using this information, can you calculate how much you will lend your friend to guarantee that you will get your money back, and the interest you are owed?

That's just what the lender does, and how they come up with the amount of money that they will lend. Lower interest rates, higher age, and a higher house value equal more money. Higher rates, lower age, and a smaller house value yield less money.

Common Questions

Reverse mortgages are relatively new, and information about them has not been easy to find until very recently. Below are some of the common questions (and answers) that are often asked about reverse mortgages.

1. How does a reverse mortgage differ from a home equity line?

   Both loans are adjustable rate mortgages, based on an index rate with a cap. A home equity line is usually repaid as interest only for a period of 5 to 10 years, and then converts to payment of principal and interest for the next 10 years. You do not have to repay a reverse mortgage as long as you live in your home.

2. If a husband and wife are 62 and 60, are they eligible for a reverse mortgage?

   No, all borrowers "on title" must be 62 or older. You would need to wait until both are 62 or remove the younger from the title in order to qualify.

Use Caution

If you remove the younger borrower from title and something happens to the older spouse, the loan becomes due. The younger borrower may have to sell the home to pay off the mortgage.

3. Is the reverse mortgage assumable, or can the loan be transferred to someone else? Can your children make payments on the loan instead of paying back as a lump sum?

   No, the loan is made to the person on title, and becomes due and payable when that person(s) leaves the home permanently, for whatever reason.

4. Can I take a reverse mortgage on a second home, such as a vacation home?

No, only the borrower's primary residence is eligible for a reverse mortgage.

5. Are reverse mortgages primarily for low-income borrowers?

   No, reverse mortgages are for senior borrowers, to allow them to tap the equity in their homes for any purpose. This can be to generate additional income, but it can also be used as an estate planning tool to shift the taxable equity in the home into nontaxable life insurance proceeds to fund long-term care policies, and so on. It is true that a smaller percentage of the home's equity is available for high-value homes.

6. Can I rent my home to someone and have a reverse mortgage?

   No, your home must be your primary residence in order to meet the terms of the reverse mortgage. Certainly you would be free to take a boarder. In the case of a multi-unit property, you can rent the other apartments, but you cannot rent out the house and go live somewhere else. This is not an investor loan.

   Some homeowners have summer and winter homes, and live part of the year in each. This is also fine, but you may take a reverse mortgage loan only on the primary residence. Generally, the primary residence is where you vote, have your bank account, file your taxes, and have your mail delivered.

7. If I take a reverse mortgage, will someone be coming over to inspect my house?

   No, generally not. If there is some reason for the lender to believe that you are no longer living in the home, such as your mail has been returned or your taxes not paid, then of course they will check up to find out why. If a complaint is lodged with the local government about the condition of the property, and the lender is notified, this will prompt them to investigate the situation.

8. Can I be turned down for a reverse mortgage?

   Yes, if the property does not meet standard requirements, if the property is in an *irrevocable trust*, or if there is some unusual problem with the title to the property. If there is a large mortgage on the house, the reverse mortgage may not yield enough money to pay it off. But if you meet the age requirements and your house is typical, then it is unlikely that you will be turned down.

9. Can I take out a home equity line after I do a reverse mortgage?

   No, but there are a few exceptions. Most lenders are not willing to be repaid after HUD (Department of Housing and Urban Development), and so will not lend money after you have taken out a reverse mortgage. There are a few that do, but typically they charge a high rate of interest.

(S) **Talk the Talk**

A **living trust** is a legal document that essentially transfers ownership of the property from the owners to a trust, which takes care of the property during the homeowner's lifetime and then distributes assets after their death, without going through probate. So the trust is on the title, not the homeowner. An **irrevocable trust** cannot be changed, and is not eligible for a reverse mortgage.

The Least You Need to Know

- Homeowners must be 62 or older to qualify for a reverse mortgage, and the home must be their primary residence.

- A reverse mortgage does not need to be repaid as long as any borrower on title continues to live in the home.

- Reverse mortgage funds may be used for any purpose.

- Reverse mortgage loans are non-recourse loans, which means that only the value of the house is used to repay the loan.

- Heirs receive any remaining equity after the loan is repaid. The bank does not "get the house."

Is a Reverse Mortgage Right for You?

In This Chapter

- Assess financial situation
- Determine future goals
- Look at alternative choices

Social Security is in trouble. The full retirement age has been pushed back. Benefits may be scaled down. The Pension Benefit Guaranty Corporation is overburdened. And the stock market, over the past few years, hasn't looked too good either.

Whether you are a senior homeowner looking for a source of additional income or a pre-retiree exploring your options, you should be aware of the reverse mortgage as an option.

Is it the right choice for you at this time, for your parents or a friend? The information that follows discusses some alternatives. If you are working with an accountant or financial advisor, talk to him or her about your current situation and options. If not, you will find some useful tools to help you assess your financial situation, your goals, and your future needs.

House Rich, Cash Poor

For many of us, our home is our largest single investment. More than half of senior homeowners own their house free and clear of any mortgage, and an additional 25 percent have only a small mortgage balance on their homes. So there is a lot of equity tied up in homes, leaving many seniors house rich, but cash poor.

Imagine your home as a big piggy bank, and the equity as the change you've saved over the years. The reverse mortgage allows you to make withdrawals of some of that money now to pay yourself.

Adding It Up—Your Finances

Do you need to raid the piggy bank? Or do you want to? And is now the right time? This is hard to determine until you take a good look at your financial situation.

It's time to make a budget. If you already have one written down, drag it out and let's use it as a starting point. Or if you're like me, I carry it around in my head. It's time to put it on paper.

Cash Flow Worksheet

Gather the bills that you have been collecting and make up a budget. Do it now. No excuses. Don't wait; don't find something else to do. Take a few minutes and fill in the cash flow sheets that follow. Begin the expenses with monthly recurring bills, such as utilities, mortgage, or other loan payments.

Include expenses that come up only periodically, such as taxes (income, real estate, and personal property), insurance premiums, and maintenance contracts for heating and air conditioning. Divide annual costs by 12 to get a monthly figure.

Under health care, remember to include co-payments and prescriptions, not just the premium costs. If you are in good health, plan on visiting the doctor at least twice a year, once for an annual check-up and once for any minor illness. If you have a chronic condition, such as arthritis, diabetes, or high blood pressure, plan on going more often: every two to three months or as your doctor suggests.

Incidental expenses are often overlooked, although they can be a large part of the budget. These might include gifts, charitable contributions, magazine subscriptions, clothing, dues, the occasional social event, and vacations.

Under cars, include an estimate for car repairs (particularly with older cars), and the cost for inspections, license plate renewals, and county stickers. If you use taxis or public transportation, include an average cost for that.

Extraordinary expenses are also often overlooked. These would be items such as a new water heater or washer, new roof, or fence. If you anticipate replacing anything major over the next five years, or remodeling the kitchen or bath, include a budget estimate for this expense as well.

What about debts? Credit cards that you are making payments on? What is the monthly amount, or what do you pay monthly?

Be realistic with your budget. It will only be useful if it is accurate.

Then list your income from all sources. This might be from a part-time job, Social Security, or pension funds. Don't forget dividends or interest earned from investments, and tax refunds.

 Good Cents

If you have a computer, you might want to consider investing in a home accounting program like Quicken or Money. Both allow you to track your expenses and income, plan a budget, manage your investments and prepare for your taxes. You can even schedule and pay bills online, if you wish. This can come in handy if you are planning to be away from home for an extended visit.

Cash Flow Worksheet

Income

Social Security   _____

Job   _____

Pension/Retirement   _____

Investments   _____

Other   _____

Total Income   _____

Expenses

Mortgage   _____

Utilities   _____

Food   _____

Clothing   _____

Taxes/Insurance   _____

Health care   _____

Auto/Transportation   _____

Incidental   _____

Credit Cards/Debt   _____

                         _____

Other   _____

Total Expenses   _____

Financial Statement

The second part of this exercise is to determine your net worth. This is simply your *assets* (what you own) minus your *liabilities* (what you owe).

List your assets. This would be anything of value that could be turned into cash if needed.

Talk the Talk

An **asset** is anything of value. Liquid assets are those that are easily turned into cash, like money market, savings or checking accounts, Certificates of Deposits, savings bonds, stocks, mutual funds, IRAs, 401k plans, or the cash value on a life insurance policy. Hard assets are those that can be sold for cash, such as your home, jewelry, furniture, artwork, antiques and collectibles, real estate, or cars.

And then list your liabilities. This would be any debt you owe or payments that you will owe in the near future, such as property or income taxes.

Financial Statement

Assets

House(s)   _____

Cars   _____

Stocks/Bonds   _____

Other Investments   _____

Checking/Savings   _____

IRA Accounts   _____

Jewelry   _____

Other   _____

                    _____

Total Assets   _____

Liabilities

Mortgage(s)   _____

Car Loans   _____

Credit Cards   _____

Income Taxes   _____

Installment Loans   _____

Other Debts   _____

                    _____

                    _____

Total Liabilities   _____

Net Worth   _____

> ($) **Talk the Talk**
>
> A **liability** is any debt you owe or may owe in the near future. Examples of liabilities are mortgage loan, car loan, student loan, credit card debt, IOU, promissory note, judgments or liens, or past-due taxes. You might want to include any bills that will be due in the near future, like your homeowner's insurance, or property or real estate taxes.

Current Versus Future Needs

You know what you make and what you spend. Take a good look at the cash flow worksheet. Are there places where you could "tighten up"? Can you move money from one category to another to make it work better for you?

The total amount of money you have to work with is what you own minus what you owe.

> **Use Caution**
>
> If the total amount of money you have to work with is zero, then it would be a good idea to go see a financial counselor. HUD offers free debt counseling, and you can find a list of these agencies on the HUD website at www.hud.gov.

So what do you imagine doing in the future? Next year? In five years? Ten years from now?

List your goals, the things you want to accomplish or would like to do. Remodel the kitchen? Fly to Europe for a week? Get a new wardrobe? Fund a long-term care plan? Help your grandchildren with college expenses?

What will this cost? Jot down the costs for items you know. Then use your worksheets to estimate the costs you don't know. Think in terms of costs per year.

Priority	Future Needs/Goals	Cost
_____	_____	_____
_____	_____	_____
_____	_____	_____
_____	_____	_____
_____	_____	_____
_____	_____	_____
_____	_____	_____
_____	_____	_____
_____	_____	_____
_____	_____	_____
_____	_____	_____
_____	_____	_____
_____	_____	_____

Add up your list. This will give you a basis for discussion with your family, accountant, and/or financial advisor. It will also give you a basis for decision making. Are you close, or is there a big gap between what you have, what you need, and what you'd like? It's certainly something to think about, and the three worksheets you've completed will give you a starting point to work with.

Lifestyle Choices

Now that you have the finances underway, it's time to look at how you want to live.

Do You Want to Stay in Your Home?

Why do you want to stay in your home? Often we keep doing the same things without really thinking about why we are doing them. If this is a home that has been in the family for years, then memories and community ties may be a very good reason to stay. But if the house needs more maintenance and upkeep than you can give it, maybe it is time to look for something easier to take care of.

Is your family local? Or have the kids and grandkids moved to other parts of the country? Have you considered selling the house and moving somewhere else? Perhaps it is time to consider it.

Moving, no matter what your age, is emotionally and physically draining. If your friends, family, or support group is here, it makes sense that you want to remain where you are. And if that is your decision, then a reverse mortgage might be part of the answer.

Five Years from Now

Look back to your list of goals and needs. Are you considering moving someplace else in the next five years? What do you envision yourself doing then?

Again, if the answer is that you want to stay where you are, then a reverse mortgage may be an answer. However, if you are looking for short-term income to tide you over, this is not a good choice.

The reverse mortgage is designed to allow seniors to tap the equity in their homes for additional income. But it is also designed to be a long-term solution. The loan is *front-end loaded*. The costs are high for a short-term solution, but very reasonable when spread out over the long term. This is how the loan was designed to be used.

 Talk the Talk

The reverse mortgage is **front-end loaded.** This means that the majority of the costs for the loan are paid at the time of closing, when you finalize the loan.

Over one to two years, the cost to borrow might be as much as 12 percent. Over 15 or 20 years, this cost is spread out and becomes a much more reasonable 3 to 5 percent, depending on loan size.

Death and Inheritance

What do you expect to happen when you die? Do your kids want to take over and live in this house? Or do they have homes of their own in other cities and towns around the country? Think about this. You might want to leave the house to them, but do the kids want it?

Sometimes the answer is yes, if this is a family home that the family shares fond memories of. Sometimes the answer is no.

And ask yourself this: What do the kids want you to do? If you are scrimping and saving to try to get by, my answer would be "please Mom/Dad, take care of yourself; I can take care of me."

I'm not waiting for my mother to die so I can get her money. I'd much rather she spend it to travel and enjoy herself. And I expect your children probably feel the same way.

If you have plenty of other investments, this is not an issue. But if the house is your single largest asset, and you are falling further and further behind, it might be time to take a good, hard look at the future.

Alternatives

You can remain in your home and keep doing what you are doing. And if that is what you want to do, it's a good choice. But if you are staying where you are because you feel you don't have any other choice, that is bad. So let's look at a couple of alternatives.

Selling the House and Moving (or Rent Back)

If your house is paid off, or nearly so, you probably have a lot of equity. If you sell the house, you will receive that equity as cash at closing. You can use these funds to buy a smaller, more affordable house, perhaps closer to family, the city, or out in the country if that is your desire.

The difference between the cost of the old and new house can be used to supplement your income, or to fund some of the items on your goals/needs list.

Another option is to sell the house, perhaps to a family member, but retain the right to continue to live in it. This is similar to the French system of *en viager* mentioned in Chapter 1.

Or you may choose to "rent back" the use of the house from your buyer. The money you received from the sale can be used for rent. This will generate a steady income for the buyer, helping them to cover the new mortgage.

Selling the house and renting it from a family member also allows you to transfer the ownership of the house to that family member, with no inheritance taxes.

Good Cents

If you sell your primary residence, you may have to pay capital gains taxes on the money made from the sale of the house. If the profit from the sale of the house is under $250,000, you may be able to exclude the profit from taxes. Talk to your accountant about this possibility and how to best structure a sale.

Assisted Living/Public Housing

If you are not able to safely live in your home anymore, or can see a time in the near future when that might be the case, it might be time to make a move, while you can still be in control of where you go. The sale of your residence would yield needed cash to pay for these services.

Or, if you simply cannot afford to live in the house anymore, you might consider public housing. Many local programs will take a portion of your income (Social Security or pension) as the "rent," in exchange for shelter in public housing. It may not be the best solution, but it is an option.

Other Programs That May Close the Gap

Call your local Agency on Aging to find out what
assistance programs may be available in your area.
They will have the most complete listing of local
programs, and are "plugged in" to the network.

Check your eligibility for SSI (Supplemental
Security Income). Many people who are eligible
don't ever file for this additional income.

If you need someone to cook an occasional meal,
Meals on Wheels is a wonderful group. In some
areas, local grocery stores will deliver. In urban
areas, Safeway has an online ordering service that
will deliver groceries to your home.

Good Cents

Certain stores and restaurants have
"senior days" when seniors get discounted
rates. This makes shopping and dining out
a bit cheaper. These are small things, but
small savings add up.

Ultimately, if you want to remain in your home
but don't have enough money, a reverse mortgage
is one way to obtain additional income to make
your life more comfortable. Loan proceeds can be
used to pay for skilled nursing care, renovations to

make it easier/safer to get around your home, or to hire someone to do heavy chores when seasons change.

The Least You Need to Know

- Identifying your goals brings you one step closer to achieving them.
- A good budget can help you achieve your goals.
- A realistic financial picture will give you the tools to make informed decisions.

Chapter 3

Single-Purpose Mortgages

In This Chapter

- The lower costs of single-purpose loans
- Limitations of single-purpose loans
- Single-purpose loans as an alternative to reverse mortgages

Reverse mortgages have flexible payment plans with no limitations on your income or the value of your home. Money from a reverse mortgage can be used for any purpose, to pay health-care costs, as income, or to renovate your home.

However, reverse mortgages can be expensive, particularly for homes valued under $100,000, and may not be suitable for all situations. Single-purpose mortgages offer a lower-cost alternative to reverse mortgages.

Single-purpose mortgages are those that are available for one specific purpose only. The most well-known single-purpose mortgage is probably a school loan. Students can take a loan for the purpose of going to school, but they do not have to begin repaying the loan until they graduate and get a job. This is referred to as deferred payment.

Some local and state governments offer single-purpose mortgages, which are available for payment of repairs and modification to your home, for property taxes, and for medical care. Typically, no payment is required for as long as you live in your home. Only two states sponsor programs that provide income to homeowners, Montana and Connecticut.

Eligibility

Eligibility requirements for a single-purpose loan vary from program to program, county to county, and state to state. Some require homeowners to be 62 or older and some limit participation to 65 or older. Most are limited to low- or moderate-income homeowners. Many programs place restrictions on the value, location, and type of property that may be eligible for a mortgage. And some programs are available only to homeowners who are partially or fully disabled, which must be certified by a doctor.

We can only talk in generalities about single-purpose loans, because most of these programs are local or county-funded programs. Each county or local government sets up programs based on what they see as a need in the community. And each local government has their own set of requirements.

In addition, local and state programs are subject to available funding and political pressure, so they change frequently. When county budgets are tight, programs may not accept new applications, eligibility requirements may be changed, or the programs may be eliminated entirely.

Deferred Payment Loans

Single-purpose loans are known by a variety of different names, but the name most commonly used is the Deferred Payment Loan or DPL, because payments on these types of loans are often deferred until some later time. DPLs are generally available for home remodeling, renovation, or, in some areas, weatherproofing the home.

DPLs differ from a home equity loan in several ways. Homeowners must demonstrate that they have good credit and sufficient income to repay a home equity loan. Since repayment is deferred, credit is generally not an issue when applying for a DPL. In addition, DPLs are often limited to homeowners with incomes 50 to 80 percent below the median income for the area. Most counties use the HUD *median* income limits. For example, the median income for 2004 for the District of Columbia was 85,400, and for Bucks County, Pennsylvania, was $68,800. So if the income were limited to 80 percent, a homeowner in the District could make no more than $17,080 and one in Bucks County could make no more than $13,760. A homeowner with income this low would not qualify for a home equity loan.

$ Talk the Talk

Every year, HUD publishes the **median** or average income for each county or Metropolitan Statistical Area (MSA). This can be found on the HUD website at http://www.huduser.org/datasets/il.html.

DPLs are the most inexpensive type of loan, with interest rates as low as 0 percent. There are generally no origination fees or mortgage insurance and closing costs are low.

Grants, sums of money that do not have to be repaid, may also be available, but generally are limited to senior homeowners beginning at various ages from 62 through 70. The paperwork to apply for DPLs can be daunting, but don't let that stop you.

There is no repayment expected on a DPL until title to the property is transferred, or the house is no longer the primary residence. In some instances, part or all of the loan balance may be "forgiven" or waived if you live in your home for a specific period of time. These are few and far between, but may be a good deal if they are available in your area.

Good Cents _____

Housing repair/modification DPLs are the most common and may be available in some areas based on income, or in Community Redevelopment zones (areas targeted for improvement), regardless of age. Grants, which do not have to be repaid, may also be available. DPLs can be used in conjunction with the HECM reverse mortgage if the DPL lender is willing to be repaid after the HECM is paid. Grants may also be used in conjunction with the reverse mortgage if the grant program allows. These programs are often not advertised or well known, so it pays to ask about any types of loans or grants that may be available.

As you can see from the income limitations, DPLs are targeted to very low-income households who probably could not afford a monthly payment. In some cases, homeowners must prove that they have tried other options before they will be allowed to apply. Local governments fund these programs as a civic duty to their citizens, and offset losses from other revenue. So funding is often limited.

Typically, *trusts* and *life estates* are not eligible for DPLs. And in most areas, current real estate and property taxes must be paid prior to application for the programs.

Talk the Talk _____

A living **trust** is a legal agreement that transfers title of the property to a third party, the trustee, during a person's lifetime. Upon their death, the trustee distributes the assets according to the trust document, without going through probate court. A **life estate** actually transfers title of the property to someone else, such as the homeowner's children, but grants the homeowner the right to use the property for their lifetime. In both cases, someone other than the homeowner is the owner of the property, which makes the property ineligible for a loan.

Let's look at one example of a widely available DPL. Rural homeowners with low incomes may be eligible for the Rural Housing Repair and Rehabilitation Loan or Grant available through the U.S. Department of Agriculture, Rural Development office. The loans are for rural homeowners unable to obtain credit elsewhere, with "very low income" (50 percent below the area's median).

Loans of up to $20,000 and grants up to $7,500 are available, to make the dwelling "more safe, sanitary, or to remove health and safety hazards." Homeowners must be 62 or older to qualify for a grant, which does not have to be repaid. For more information on this program, contact the USDA Rural

Development office in your area. Information may also be found on the agency's website at www. rurdev.usda.gov.

Reverse Annuity Mortgage

A reverse annuity mortgage is similar in many respects to a reverse mortgage. The home's value is used to determine the amount of the loan, and the loan does not have to be repaid until the home-owner dies or leaves the home. Payments are available for a specific period of time, 5 to 10 years.

Two states currently offer specialized reverse annuity mortgages: Montana and Connecticut. They have been included in this chapter because they have very specific limitations on income and age of homeowners. And in the case of Connecticut, the loan is available for one very specific use only.

Montana

The Reverse Annuity Mortgage (RAM) has been in existence since 1989 and is available to Montana state residents only. Residents must be 68 years of age or older, and their income must be less than 200 percent of the median poverty level.

For example, the poverty level for a one-person household in 2004 was $9,310. So a single home-owner would have to make less than $18,620 to qualify.

The loan limit is 80 percent of the FHA estimated value for the home, with a maximum loan amount of $100,000. The interest rate is fixed. Homeowners receive monthly payments for 10 years. At the end of this period payments stop, but the loan does not have to be repaid as long as the homeowner continues to live in the home.

For more information, contact the Montana Board of Housing at 800-761-6264 or visit their website at www.housing.state.mt.us.

Connecticut

Connecticut also offers a Reverse Mortgage annuity, which is limited to Connecticut residents 70 years of age or older who have some long-term care costs. An independent certification of this condition is required.

The loan is limited to 70 percent of the home's value. Property types are limited to single family homes, condominiums, and planned unit developments. Monthly payments can be made over a 5- or 10-year period, and repayment is expected when the borrower(s) die or cease to occupy the home. To qualify, the income of the homeowner must be $75,400 a year or lower.

For more information, contact the Connecticut Housing Finance Authority at 860-571-3502, or visit the website at www.chfa.org.

Property Tax Deferrals

A good portion of local and county government budgets is from real estate and property taxes. And in most counties, there is some form of property tax rebate, credit, or abatement available for low-income seniors. Again, guidelines vary as to age and income level, and most must be applied for every tax year.

In addition, some state and local governments offer a "property tax deferral" loan, which can be used by seniors to pay only their yearly property taxes. These are generally offered at a low interest rate and have eligibility rules for income and age.

Most of the programs have a cap, which limits the total amount of the loan over the borrower's lifetime. Once reached, the borrower can no longer apply for this exemption. Most programs will not allow you to combine them with another reverse mortgage loan, such as the HECM.

Costs for this type of loan are generally low, and the interest rate is fixed. Most allow the loan to be repaid when the house is sold or the borrower ceases to occupy the house.

A study by the AARP in 2000 showed that some form of property tax deferral was available in 24 states and the District of Columbia. Contact your local tax authority to find out what may be available in your area.

Digging for Gold

Perhaps the biggest challenge to getting a single-purpose mortgage is finding out about it in the first place. It's like digging for gold: a lot of hard work, but the reward can be worth the trouble.

Single-purpose loans are generally established by local government agencies to address a specific need, such as a rise in unpaid property taxes among low-income households. A loan for the purpose of paying unpaid property taxes might be handled through the local taxing agency, through the county finance office, or through the housing office.

To make matters more difficult, single-purpose mortgage loans are known by a variety of different names. Among the most common are Deferred Payment Loans (DPLs), Reverse Annuity Mortgages (RAMs), Property Tax Deferral loans (PTDs), and Enterprise Zones and Community Redevelopment loans. These are just a few of the names and acronyms you may stumble across in your search for alternatives to reverse mortgages.

Don't mention "reverse mortgage." If you do, you will probably be directed back to information on the HECM and Home Keeper.

Don't give up. Keep digging. Unless you run across an unusually well-informed employee, you will have to call each agency individually. Start with the list that follows:

- **Local Tax Authority.** Check for property tax deferrals, senior exemptions, or Property Tax Deferral loans.

- **Local Housing Authority.** Check for Enterprise or Community Redevelopment loans. These are loans for areas of the community the county wishes to improve. Low-interest loans and special tax rebates may be available in these neighborhoods. Also ask about home repair or improvement loans or grants for seniors.

- **Agency on Aging.** Ask about any special programs for seniors or homeowners with disabilities. This department will have also information on medical programs and in-home nursing aid programs available for seniors.

- **Local HUD Counseling Agencies.** Offers debt, pre-foreclosure and reverse mortgage counseling, among other things. The local counselors are generally "plugged in" and aware of the most current programs available in the area. There is no cost for initial counseling services.

Keep asking questions. Check back with the local agencies from time to time. Remember that local government programs can change frequently. There are a lot of resources out there, but you have to be willing to dig to find them.

Good Cents

An often overlooked opportunity is the local utility companies. Many offer deferred or reduced payment plans for seniors for renovation and utilities. Many also offer a budget plan to spread energy costs evenly over a 12-month period.

The Least You Need to Know

- Single-purpose loans are known by a variety of names.
- Single-purpose loans have very specific eligibility requirements, and restrictions on the use of the funds.
- Single-purpose loans have limited funding and only a few homeowners will qualify for these loans.

Home Equity Conversion Mortgage

In This Chapter

- What a Home Equity Conversion Mortgage (HECM) is
- How the HECM differs from other reverse mortgages
- HECM payment options
- Future changes to HECM

The Home Equity Conversion Mortgage (HECM) is the most popular of the reverse mortgage programs, because of its relatively large loan sizes, its flexible payment programs, and its choice of interest rate options. This chapter explains how the HECM works, and what the payment and interest rate options are.

The Popular Favorite

The HECM is an FHA-insured reverse mortgage designed to allow older homeowners to tap the equity in their homes to generate cash without having to sell the home.

The HECM is the most popular reverse mortgage program because it often generates the most cash for low- and moderate-priced homes. This is largely due to the FHA insurance. This insures that the homeowner will be paid, even if the lender defaults. It also insures that the lender will receive full repayment of the loan, even if the value of the house is less than the total amount of the loan.

The HECM has several payment plans, which makes it very flexible. These include a lump sum at closing, a credit line, and monthly payments. These can be combined to create a customized payment plan to suit each homeowner's needs. Payment plans can be changed in the future, generally for a small fee.

One significant drawback is that the amount of the loan may be limited by the FHA maximum loan limit. Limits vary from county to county and state to state. Generally, FHA limits are 87 percent of the conforming limit set by Fannie Mae in high-cost areas, and 48 percent in low-cost areas. Limits are set annually.

For 2005, single-family limits are $312,895 for high-cost areas and $172,632 for low-cost areas. Alaska, Hawaii, Guam and the U.S. Virgin Islands may have limits up to 50 percent higher.

Eligibility

All borrowers must be 62 years or older, and must occupy the property as their primary residence. If a younger spouse or older child is on the title to the property, then they must be removed in order to proceed with the loan.

 Use Caution

> If there is a financial need, you may wish to consider having a younger spouse removed from the title to proceed with the loan. It is possible that a reverse mortgage can be refinanced at a later point to add the younger spouse, but this will depend on the house value, interest rates, and loan balance at that time. There may not be enough money available to accomplish this. And if the older spouse dies, the younger spouse will have to pay off the reverse mortgage at that time. Consider the potential consequences carefully.

Borrowers must own their homes, or have mortgage balances small enough to be paid off by the reverse mortgage. Any liens or judgments, such as back-due property taxes, must also be cleared. However, both can be paid with proceeds from the HECM at closing.

All borrowers must obtain HECM counseling, which is provided at no cost by HUD-trained counselors. Counseling certificates are valid for 180 days.

The property must be your primary residence. Eligible properties are one- to four-unit properties, or units in a condominium or planned unit development (PUD). Manufactured homes, condos, and PUDs must be FHA-approved.

Properties held in living trusts may be eligible if all borrowers and the trust meets HUD guidelines. All borrowers involved with the trust must obtain counseling.

There are no credit or income qualifications for the HECM. However, your credit will be checked for any outstanding liens or judgments. If you have defaulted on any government loan, there is a waiting period during which you may be ineligible for the HECM loan.

How Much Can You Borrow?

The maximum you can borrow, known as the "principal limit" of the loan, is determined by …

- The age of the youngest borrower
- The appraised value or maximum claim amount, whichever is lower
- The expected average interest rate

The loan term, how long the loan will continue, is based on the borrower's age. The younger you are, the longer you are likely to live, and the longer the loan must be held. So the age of the youngest borrower is the basis for the loan. There is no adjustment made for the number of borrowers. A single man or woman and a couple will both get the same amount.

The appraised value is the "most likely" value for your home as determined by an independent evaluation. If the value of your home is more than the FHA maximum claim amount, the maximum claim amount is used to calculate the principal limit of the loan.

The FHA maximum claim amount tends to be higher in urban areas and lower in rural areas. So if we look at the example of a $280,000 house in Washington, D.C., the value of $280,000 would be used to calculate the loan. In rural Pennsylvania, the same house may be limited to the maximum claim amount of $172,632.

The principal limit is the maximum amount that you will be allowed to borrow. Based on an 8 percent expected average interest rate, the principal limit for the 62-year-old borrower in D.C. would be $106,960. In rural Pennsylvania, the principal limit would be $65,945.

The "expected average interest rate" is the 10-year Treasury bill rate, plus the margin set by Fannie Mae, at the time the loan is signed. This is an estimate of what the interest rates may be over an extended period of time. So the expected rate will always be higher than your starting interest rate, which is based on the 1-year Treasury bill rate.

The following table shows the effect of age and the expected average interest rates for a house value of $172,632 (based on the HECM with a monthly adjustment). The highest principal limit will be available to the oldest borrowers when rates are lowest.

		Age		
	62	72	82	92
6%	$98,918	$115,491	$133,712	$149,672
7%	$80,792	$100,817	$123,087	$143,975
8%	$65,945	$87,697	$113,247	$138,106
9%	$54,034	$76,303	$104,097	$132,409

Choosing an Interest Rate

The previous table refers to the HECM monthly adjustment. A choice of interest rate options is an additional feature of the HECM loan. Borrowers can choose either a monthly adjustable or yearly adjustable rate. Both are based on the 1-year Treasury bill rate, plus a margin. (Refer to Chapter 1 for a variable rate primer.)

The monthly adjustable rate is calculated as the 1-year Treasury bill rate plus a margin of 1.5 percent:

1-year T Bill + 1.5% = Initial Interest Rate

4.5% + 1.5% = 6%

Each month on your anniversary date, the rate will be changed as the T-bill rises and falls. The rate increase is "capped" at 10 percent over the initial rate at closing. So if your initial interest rate is 6 percent, the interest rate cannot exceed 16 percent.

Will it go this high? Over the last 15 years, loan rates have remained under 10 percent (using current margin of 1.5%). So it is not likely, but if we experience high inflation it is possible.

In most cases, the monthly adjustable rate provides a slightly higher loan amount because the initial interest rate for the monthly adjustment is lower than the annual adjustment rate.

The annual adjustable rate is also determined at closing and will change on the anniversary date of the loan each year. The current margin is 3.1 percent, 1.6 percent higher than the monthly adjustment:

1-year T Bill + 3.1% = Initial Interest Rate

4.5% + 3.1% = 7.6%

The lifetime cap for the annual adjustment is "capped" at 5 percent over the start rate, half that of the monthly adjustable. So if the initial rate is 7.6 percent, the interest rate cannot exceed 12.6 percent over the life of the loan.

In either case, future increases have no effect on the payments you receive or the principal loan amount, which is established upon closing the loan. However, a change in rates will affect the loan balance, which will grow more quickly if rates rise, and more slowly if they fall.

If there is little difference between the annual and monthly adjustment, then you might consider the annual rate for the lower cap. If you are looking for the most money you can receive, the monthly adjustable is usually the better choice.

How Much Will it Cost?

Once the principal limit has been determined, closing costs and fees for insurance, origination, and servicing will be deducted. These may also be paid in cash at closing, if you prefer.

As a general rule of thumb, expect about 6 percent of the value of the home (or FHA limit, whichever is lower) will be charged as closing costs. This holds true for houses $150,000 and higher. For houses under that value, the percentage is often higher as some closing costs are fixed. For example, an appraisal costs between $300 and $500 for a single family home. The price does not change because the home is worth less.

On a loan comparison, you will generally see fees broken down as the *service set-aside*, mortgage insurance, origination fee, and closing costs. In some cases, the mortgage insurance, fees, and closing costs will be lumped together. But let's take a look at them individually.

Service Set-Aside

The lender will charge a monthly servicing fee to monitor the loan. For the HECM with a monthly adjustment, this can be no more than $35/month. For the annual adjustment, the fee is limited to $30/month.

Talk the Talk

The **service set-aside** is an amount that is literally "set aside," or subtracted from the principal limit to cover the cost of the fee over the life of the loan. Interest is not charged on this amount until the servicing fee is actually used each month. It is not actually put in an account somewhere, but is removed on paper from the loan amount calculations.

The amount of the service set-aside will be determined by your age and the actual service fee charged for this service by the lender.

Mortgage Insurance

All HECM loans are FHA-insured, as stated earlier. There is an initial upfront premium of 2 percent, which is based on the value of the home or the FHA limit, whichever is lower. For our example of $172,632, the upfront premium would be

$3,452.64. This is collected when the loan closes, and can be financed as part of the loan.

The second cost is an annual premium of ½ of a percent. This is divided into 12 increments and charged monthly to your loan balance.

Origination Fee

The origination fee is charged by the lender to cover the costs to prepare and handle the loan application. HUD limits the origination fee to $2,000 or 2 percent of the maximum claim amount, whichever is greater.

Closing Costs

Closing costs cover the fees and services required to originate and close your loan. Most of these are "third-party" charges, or costs paid to other organizations or government agencies. Closing costs will vary, depending on your state, county, and the location of your home. These may include …

- Credit report ($10–$40).
- Appraisal ($300–$500).
- Flood certification ($10–$30).
- Recording fees (varies by county/state).
- Title insurance (varies by county/state—often the most expensive item on Good Faith Estimate).
- Endorsements on title insurance ($100–$400, depending on the state).

- Attorney's or settlement fee ($150–$800).
- Title exam and binder ($225–$400).
- State and county taxes (varies).
- Document preparation ($100–$250).

You can pay any or all of the fees, except the service set-aside, in cash at closing, or you can finance these as part of the loan. If you choose to finance the costs, interest and the cost for mortgage insurance will increase your loan amount.

Payment Options

One of the nicest features of the HECM is the flexibility of the payment features. The loan has five possible payment plans, which can be combined to suit the borrower's needs. These are …

- **Tenure.** An annuity-type payment for as long as borrower(s) live in their home.
- **Term.** A monthly payment for a specific time period.
- **Line of Credit.** A line of credit that can grow in value and that you can draw as needs arise.
- **Modified Term.** Combining a lump sum or line of credit with a monthly payment for a specific time period.
- **Modified Tenure.** Combining a lump sum or line of credit with a monthly payment for as long as borrower(s) live in their home.

In Texas, state law prohibits the use of the line of credit.

The tables that follow in the payment sections illustrate what a typical payment might be, assuming an expected average interest rate of 8 percent, with closing costs of $2000 mortgage insurance, $2,000 or 2 percent origination fee, and closing costs of $2,000. For annual adjustment, average rate was estimated at 9.6 percent.

Tenure

Borrowers choosing the tenure option will receive equal monthly payments for as long the borrowers maintain the home as their primary residence. In the case of a husband and wife, only one borrower needs to remain in the home. The payment is smaller than if chosen for a specified period (say 10 years), but the payment is ongoing.

The payment remains fixed, based on the estimated payment on the day you signed the loan paperwork. But there is no possibility that you will "outlive" the payments.

The first table, Typical Monthly Tenure Payments/ HECM Monthly, illustrates what a typical monthly payment might be with an interest rate of 8 percent. The second table, Typical Monthly Tenure Payments/HECM Annual, illustrates what the typical tenure payment would be at 9.6 percent.

Typical Monthly Tenure Payments/ HECM Monthly

| | Maximum Claim Limit | | | |
	$50,000	$100,000	$150,000	$200,000
Age				
62	$74	$207	$332	$458
72	$130	$321	$504	$687
82	$226	$519	$803	$1,087
92	$520	$1,134	$1,731	$2,329

Typical Monthly Tenure Payments/ HECM Annual

| | Maximum Claim Limit | | | |
	$50,000	$100,000	$150,000	$200,000
Age				
62	$46	$56	$257	$358
72	$106	$278	$441	$605
82	$210	$491	$761	$1,032
92	$504	$1,105	$1,688	$2,272

Term Option

Borrowers that want a specific sum of money monthly could choose the term plan. You specify the term (again, take 10 years), and you will receive equal payments based on the amount available at closing for 10 years. At the end of that period payments cease, as there is no more money to draw on.

Or if you want a specific sum monthly, you can specify that amount and payments will continue until funds are exhausted. In either case, you will not have to repay the loan until you move, die, or sell the home.

Typically, the term payments will be higher than tenure payments. However, for the oldest borrowers, this is not true. Because payments are calculated based on an average age of 100, the oldest borrowers will receive higher monthly payments if they choose tenure payments.

The following table, Typical Monthly Term Payments/HECM Monthly for 10 Years, shows what the typical monthly payments would be over a 10-year period for the Monthly HECM option at 8 percent. The second table, Typical Monthly Term Payments/HECM Annual for 10 Years, shows the payments for the Annual HECM option at 9.6 percent.

Typical Monthly Term Payments/HECM Monthly for 10 Years

| | Maximum Claim Limit | | | |
	$50,000	$100,000	$150,000	$200,000
Age				
62	$123	$346	$557	$767
72	$204	$504	$729	$1,081
82	$302	$694	$1,073	$1,452
92	$407	$889	$1,355	$1,823

Typical Monthly Term Payments/HECM Annual for 10 Years

| | Maximum Claim Limit | | | |
	$50,000	$100,000	$150,000	$200,000
Age				
62	$70	$239	$395	$551
72	$157	$410	$650	$890
82	$271	$634	$983	$1,333
92	$402	$880	$1,345	$1,811

Line of Credit

This is one of the nicest features of the HECM loan. The available balance of the loan can be placed in a line of credit, from which you can draw funds as needed.

This works in much the same way as a home equity line of credit. Interest is not charged on the amount available, only the amount drawn out for your use. One big difference is how you access your money. Currently, you will not receive a credit card or checks. Instead, you must send or fax a letter to the lender requesting whatever amount you require. The minimum draw amount is $500.

The balance that remains in the credit line will grow at approximately the same rate the loan is being charged at, plus the ½ of a percent mortgage insurance. So if rates are 5.5 percent, plus the ½ of a percent mortgage insurance, you will earn 6 percent in the credit line. This is a better rate than most banks, CDs, or money markets.

Use Caution

> Before the loan comes due, draw all funds out of the credit line. Funds left in the credit line will not be counted toward the loan payoff, and you will not be able to access the money until after the loan is repaid. So if you don't draw the money out, you will have to come up with an equal amount of cash to satisfy the loan.

The following table, Typical Credit Line or Lump Sum Payments/HECM Monthly, illustrates what the lump sum or credit line amount might be if the interest rate on the HECM Monthly option is 8 percent. The second table, Typical Credit Line or Lump Sum Payments/HECM Annual, shows the loan amounts and ages for the HECM Annual option at 9.6 percent.

Typical Credit Line or Lump Sum Payments/ HECM Monthly

| | Maximum Claim Limit | | | |
	$50,000	$100,000	$150,000	$200,000
Age				
62	$10,020	$28,120	$45,220	$62,320
72	$16,568	$40,968	$64,368	$87,768
82	$24,545	$56,345	$87,145	$117,945
92	$33,092	$72,092	$110,092	$148,092

Typical Credit Line or Lump Sum Payments/ HECM Annual

| | Maximum Claim Limit | | | |
	$50,000	$100,000	$150,000	$200,000
Age				
62	$5,343	$18,183	$30,043	$41,843
72	$11,893	$31,143	$41,393	$67,643
82	$20,806	$48,156	$74,706	$101,256
92	$30,533	$68,883	$102,233	$137,583

You can draw all or part of the loan funds after closing for any purpose you wish—to pay off existing bills or to get rid of the payment for an existing mortgage. Like any refinance, the HECM allows a three-day right of rescission period. You have three days to change your mind before the loan is "funded" and you receive your money.

Good Cents

If you have an immediate need for funds, request a lump sum at closing. It often takes several weeks or more before the credit line is set up and available for your use.

Modified Plans

You can choose a combination of the lump sum payment or line of credit and either the tenure or term payments. You can take a lump sum to weatherproof the house at closing, and then have tenure payments set up for the balance. Or you might want to set aside some money in the credit line for unforeseen expenses, such as a new car or furnace, and set up a payment plan for the balance. The choice is yours.

In addition, you can change the payment plan at any point in time. If you have chosen the credit line but find that you need money on a regular basis, you can change it. Generally the lender will charge a small fee to make the switch ($20–$30). And you can change the plan as many times as you wish, as long as there is money in the account.

Future Changes

One of the most significant expected changes to the HUD guidelines is the decision to allow borrowers to "lock" the initial interest rate when they make their loan application. However, policy makers are still working on how this will be implemented, and it is likely to be some time before this is put into practice.

Another recent change allows for changes in the way refinancing of HECM mortgages are handled. The new ruling limits the mortgage insurance to 2 percent of the difference between the old maximum claim amount and the new maximum claim amount. As shown in the following, savings can add up:

(New claim amount – old claim amount) × 2% = MIP

For example:

($200,000 – $100,000) × 2% = $2,000

Versus new loan $200,000 × 2% = $4,000

You might want to consider refinancing an older HECM if your property value has increased significantly, as they have recently in many metropolitan areas. Payments are set at the initial signing date, so older loans may have smaller payments than borrowers can receive today.

The decision regarding refinances was issued by HUD in April of 2004, and Fannie Mae has just agreed to purchase these loans in 2005.

The Least You Need to Know

- The HECM offers more flexible payment plans than other reverse mortgage options.

- In most cases, homeowners will receive a larger loan from the HECM than from other reverse mortgages.

- There are two interest rate options for the HECM, one that adjusts monthly and one that adjusts annually. The monthly adjustment yields a larger loan amount.

- The costs for a HECM are higher than for a Home Keeper, but the loan amount is also generally higher.

Home Keeper

In This Chapter

- Differences between Home Keeper and Home Equity Conversion Mortgage (HECM)
- Purchasing power with Home Keeper
- Home Keeper costs
- Typical payment plans of Home Keeper
- Loans on properties not allowed by FHA

The Home Keeper is similar in many respects to the HECM, but its differences are intriguing. The costs are lower than the HECM, but it also generally provides a small loan amount. There are certain instances where it does beat the HECM, so it should always be considered. One special feature of the Home Keeper is that it can be used to purchase a property as well—not just refinance a home you own. That is an intriguing possibility.

The Home Keeper

The Home Keeper is Fannie Mae's proprietary reverse mortgage loan. Like the Home Equity Conversion Mortgage (HECM), it is designed to allow older homeowners to tap the equity in their homes to generate additional income.

Although the loans are similar, the Home Keeper has its own unique features. As well as refinancing, the Home Keeper can be used for purchasing a home. The property restrictions for the Home Keeper are less stringent than FHA's, so some properties may be eligible for the Home Keeper that might otherwise be excluded under FHA guidelines.

Fannie Mae establishes a national lending limit yearly. For 2005, the maximum loan amount for single family homes is $359,650. Alaska, Hawaii, Guam, and the U.S. Virgin Islands may have limits up to 50 percent higher.

Eligibility

All borrowers must be 62 years or older and must occupy the property as their primary residence. Fannie Mae limits the number of borrowers to three.

Like the HECM, borrowers must own their homes, or have mortgage balances small enough to be paid off by the reverse mortgage. Liens and judgments against the title to the property must be cleared at closing, but can be paid from the loan proceeds.

All borrowers must obtain counseling, which is provided at no cost by a Fannie Mae counselor. The counselor is required to discuss the differences between the Home Keeper and HECM, and provide you with examples of both.

Eligible properties are single-family homes, one-unit homes, or units in a condominium or planned unit development (PUD). Condominium and PUD units must be approved by Fannie Mae.

Good Cents _____

In condominium complexes, only 10 percent of all loans in the complex can be FHA loans, conventional or HECM. Fannie Mae allows 20 percent of all loans in one complex to be Fannie Mae loans. So if the condominium is not eligible for a HECM loan because of the number of loans, it may be eligible for a Home Keeper.

Properties held in trusts may be eligible, if the trust meets Fannie Mae guidelines. If your property is a condo, PUD, or in a trust, you should request that these are pre-approved before you proceed with an appraisal or inspections.

How Much Can You Borrow?

The maximum you can borrow, known as the "principal limit" of the loan, is determined by …

- The age and number of borrower(s), and
- The appraised value or maximum claim amount, whichever is lower.

The loan term, how long the loan will continue, is based on the borrower's age. Younger borrowers will live longer, so the loan term is expected to be longer.

Good Cents

If you have not talked to your family about taking a reverse mortgage, now would be an ideal time. It is a good idea to include whoever will be your executor, so they know what you are doing and what you expect to happen after you die. This will also give your children a chance to ask questions and the opportunity to become comfortable with the loan guidelines.

The Home Keeper also considers the number of borrowers. Statistically, couples live longer than individuals. So two borrowers will receive less money than one.

Again, the appraised value is the "most likely" value for your home as determined by an independent evaluation. If the value of your home is higher than the lending limit, then the lending limit will be the maximum claim amount used to calculate the principal limit of the loan.

Fannie Mae's Home Keeper is self-insured, so it is also a "non-recourse" loan. No more than the value of the house may be used in repayment.

Unlike the HECM, interest rates do not play a role in the calculation of the loan balance.

So let's assume that closing costs are financed and that you have a house worth $300,000. A 72-year-old single man living in Washington, D.C., could receive a lump sum of $103,038. A couple in the same house would get $125,518.

Interest Rates

The interest rate for the Home Keeper is based on the 1-month *Certificate of Deposit rate* (CD *index rate*). The current margin is 3.4 percent. So the rate is calculated as:

> 1-month CD index + 3.4% = Initial Interest Rate

or:

> 3.5% + 3.4% = 6.9%

($) **Talk the Talk** _____

> The **index rate** used by Fannie Mae
> is the weekly average of the 1-month
> **Certificate of Deposit rates.** The 1-month
> CD rate is equivalent to the average rate
> you would get if you put your money in a
> 30-day CD.

Each month on the anniversary date of the loan
closing, the rate will change, as the CD index
rises and falls. The rate increase is "capped" at
12 percent over the initial rate at closing. So if
your initial interest rate is 6.9 percent, the interest
rate cannot exceed 18.9 percent.

How Much Will it Cost?

After the principal limit has been determined,
closing costs and fees for origination and servicing
will be deducted. These may also be paid in cash at
closing, if you prefer.

As a general rule of thumb, expect about 4 percent
of the value of the home (or the maximum loan
amount, whichever is lower) to be charged as closing costs. For houses with low values, the percentage of costs is considerably higher.

Good Cents _____

For homes with values of under
$100,000, the percentage of closing
costs to the loan value will be higher.
The origination fee is 2 percent or
$2,000, whichever is lower. Many of
the closing costs are fixed costs, such as
the appraisal, credit report, and settlement
fee. It would cost a minimum of $3500
to close, and for a $50,000 house, the
closing costs would be 7 percent of the
house's value.

Service Set-Aside

The lender will charge a monthly servicing fee to
monitor the loan. This will be between $15 and
$30 per month. An amount is "set aside," or sub-
tracted from the principal limit, to cover the cost
of the fee over the life of the loan. Interest is not
charged on this amount until the servicing fee is
actually used each month.

The amount of the service set-aside will be determined by your age and the actual service fee
charged by the lender for this service.

Mortgage Insurance

Fannie Mae self-insures the Home Keeper loan,
so there is no separate fee charged for mortgage
insurance.

Origination Fee

The origination fee is charged by the lender to cover the costs to prepare and handle the loan application. Fannie Mae limits the origination fee to $2,000 or 2 percent of the annual lending limit, whichever is greater.

Closing Costs

Closing costs cover the fees and services required to originate and close your loan. These are essentially the same as those charged for the HECM loan, so refer to that section of the previous chapter for typical costs. As a general rule, expect closing costs to be 1 percent of the house value or loan amount, whichever is lower if the house value is above $150,000. In high-cost states, this may be higher.

You can pay any or all of the fees, except the service set-aside, in cash at closing, or you can finance these as part of the loan. If you choose to finance the costs, the interest and the cost for mortgage insurance will increase your loan amount.

Payment Options

The Home Keeper mortgage allows you to choose one of three options for payment plans. These are …

- **Tenure.** An annuity-type payment for as long as borrower(s) live in their home.

- **Line of Credit.** An income-bearing line of credit, from which the borrower can draw as needs arise.
- **Modified Tenure.** Combining a lump sum or line of credit with a monthly payment for as long as borrower(s) live in their home.

In Texas, state law prohibits the use of the line of credit.

The tables that follow illustrate what typical tenure payments might be, assuming closing costs of 1 percent and an origination fee of 2 percent, both of which are financed. The first table, Typical Monthly Tenure Payments/Single Borrower, shows the estimated payments for a single person. The second table, Typical Monthly Tenure Payments/Couple, shows the payments for any two people, perhaps a married couple or relatives sharing a house. You will notice that the payments for a single borrower are higher.

Typical Monthly Tenure Payments/ Single Borrower

	House Value			
	$200,000	**$250,000**	**$300,000**	**$350,000**
Age				
62	$234	$300	$366	$433
72	$548	$693	$838	$982
82	$949	$1,194	$1,439	$1,683
92	$1,361	$1,708	$2,056	$2,404

Typical Monthly Tenure Payments/Couple

| | House Value | | | |
	$200,000	$250,000	$300,000	$350,000
Age				
62	$212	$273	$333	$394
72	$347	$441	$535	$629
82	$739	$931	$1,123	$1,316
92	$1,180	$1,482	$1,785	$2,087

A line of credit with the lump sum of the loan can be established for your convenience. Interest is not charged until the funds are drawn out of the credit line. Unlike the HECM, the credit line for the Home Keeper does not grow in value.

Use Caution

The line of credit is a "revolving" line, which means that you can draw money out and pay it back at any point in time. You might choose to do this to keep funds available or to keep the interest charges low. If you repay the loan in full (pay interest and any borrowed funds), then the loan will automatically terminate. This is true for both the Home Keeper and the HECM.

Typical Credit Line/Lump Sum/Single Borrower

	House Value			
	$200,000	**$250,000**	**$300,000**	**$350,000**
Age				
62	$28,607	$36,675	$44,742	$52,810
72	$67,462	$87,250	$103,038	$180,223
82	$101,608	$127,813	$154,018	$180,223
92	$122,145	$153,355	$184,564	$215,774

Typical Credit Line/Lump Sum/Couple

	House Value			
	$200,000	**$250,000**	**$300,000**	**$350,000**
Age				
62	$17,229	$22,145	$27,061	$31,977
72	$40,826	$51,916	$63,006	$74,096
82	$83,877	$105,697	$127,518	$149,338
92	$119,915	$150,656	$181,397	$212,138

Home Keeper vs. HECM

If you compare the tenure or credit line payments between the Home Keeper and the HECM, in most cases, the HECM will be higher. However, this is only part of the puzzle.

The Home Keeper has a national lending limit. Higher-priced houses in more rural areas are often penalized by the lower geographic limits on FHA loans.

Let's assume a house value of $350,000. Assume closing costs of $3,500, mortgage insurance, and origination fees of 2 percent. The closing costs, mortgage insurance, and origination fees will be financed for both loans. The expected average interest rate for the HECM loan will be 8 percent with monthly adjustment. (Note: You will not pay mortgage insurance for the Home Keeper.)

A single man, age 72, in Washington, D.C., could receive $120,826 from the Home Keeper, or tenure payments of $982. He would receive $138,478 or $1084/month from the HECM.

But let's take this same borrower and place him in rural Pennsylvania. In this area, the FHA maximum claim amount comes into play, at approximately $186,000. His loan amount from the Home Keeper will remain the same at $120,826 or $982/month. The HECM would yield $79,768 or $624/month. In this instance, the Home Keeper is the clear winner.

The FHA has strict property guidelines (see Chapters 7 and 8 for details). If a property does not pass the FHA's stringent criteria, and an older home might not meet FHA's safety requirements, the same property might qualify for the Home Keeper.

The Least You Need to Know

- Home Keeper does not use interest rates to calculate loan amounts.

- A single person always gets a higher loan payment than a couple.

- Compare the Home Keeper and the HECM loans before you make a decision about which one is best for you.

- A property that does not qualify for the HECM due to property issues may qualify for the Home Keeper.

Chapter 6

Cash Account

In This Chapter

- Cash Accounts are appropriate high-value properties
- Closing costs for Cash Accounts
- Limited payment options for Cash Accounts
- Cash Accounts can be used to purchase property

One company, Financial Freedom, a subsidiary of IndyMac Bank, F.S.B., offers a proprietary line of reverse mortgage products named the Cash Account. These are specifically designed for high-value properties.

These "jumbo" loans are available with a variety of closing-cost options. They generally provide a loan amount of less than one third the value of the property. Payment plans are limited and are determined by the closing-cost option chosen.

In this chapter, the eligibility requirements for the Cash Accounts are reviewed, along with borrowing limits, the fees associated with the loans, and the different loan options. At the end of the chapter, a comparison shows the difference between the HECM, Home Keeper, and the Cash Account.

Eligibility

To qualify for a Cash Account loan, borrowers must be 62 years or older and must occupy the property as their primary residence.

The borrowers must own their homes or have mortgage balances small enough to be paid off by the reverse mortgage. Liens and judgments against the title to the property must be cleared at closing, but can be paid from the loan proceeds.

All borrowers must obtain counseling, which is provided at no cost by counselors employed by the lender. Counseling is performed over the telephone and is completed during the loan process, rather than before it starts.

Counseling, like that offered for the HECM and Home Keeper, is to ensure that the customer understands how the loan works, how the interest rate is adjusted, how the property is valued, and what the expected loan amount will be. Financial Freedom applies the same stringent controls to its proprietary product line that it exercises with the HECM and Home Keeper loans.

Eligible properties are single-family homes, 1- to 4-unit properties (as long as the borrower(s) lives in one unit), condominiums, Planned Unit Developments (PUDs), and manufactured homes. High-value co-ops in New York are also eligible. Co-ops in other areas are being considered.

The Cash Account is not available in all states. Check with the loan officer you are working with to see if your state is eligible.

Interest Rates

The interest rate for the Cash Account is a variable rate, and is calculated in the same manner as that for the HECM and Home Keeper loans. The interest rate for the Cash Account products is based on the 6-month *Libor rate*, plus a margin of 5 percent, as shown in the following:

> 6-month Libor rate + Margin = Initial Interest Rate

For example, if the Libor rate is 3.5%, the interest rate is:

> 3.5% + 5% = 8.5%

 Talk the Talk

The **Libor rate** is the London InterBank Offered Rate. It is the rate that banks in the London market offer to lend each other money.

The interest rate is capped at 6 percent above the start rate. So if start rate is 8.5 percent, it cannot exceed 14.5 percent over the life of the loan.

For the first six months, the loans feature an introductory rate that is ½ percent lower than the current rate.

How Much Can You Borrow?

The maximum you can borrow, known as the "principal limit" of the loan, is determined by …

- The age and number of borrower(s), and
- The appraised value of the property.

The chart that follows, Typical Lump Sum Payments, is based on a $1,000,000 property. The difference between a single person and a couple is fairly large in the younger years, but narrows as the borrower's age increases.

Typical Lump Sum Payments

Single	Age	Couple
$168,000	62	$120,600
$282,500	72	$224,000
$438,400	82	$352,600
$567,700	92	$514,100

The loan term, how long the loan will continue, is based on the borrower's age. Younger borrowers will live longer, so the loan term is expected to be longer. A couple will get a smaller loan balance than a single man. Statistics show that couples live longer, and generally one is younger than the other.

The appraised value is the "most likely" value for your home as determined by an independent evaluation. There is no maximum value for Cash Account loans, but there is a minimum value of $75,000.

Cash Account loans are not government-insured, but they are non-recourse loans backed by the lender's investors. As with the HECM and Home Keeper loans, only the cost of the home will be used to repay the loan. If the value of the home is less than the loan value at the time of the home-owner's death or sale of the home, then only the home's value is due.

So let's use the Simply Zero loan with no state or local taxes and a home value of $1,000,000. A 72-year-old single man living in Washington, D.C., could receive a lump sum of $282,500. A couple in the same house would get $224,000.

Fees

There are three loans in the Cash Account family. These are the standard Cash Account, the Zero Point and the Simply Zero loans.

The closing costs and payment options will be determined by which Cash Account product you choose. A servicing fee of $30/month is added to the loan balance, except where prohibited by law.

For homes valued at $500,000 and less, the lender will collect a $350 fee for the appraisal. The fee will be $500 if the home is valued over $500,000. This will be an FHA appraisal chosen from a list of appraisers approved by the lender.

For homes valued over $2,000,000, a second appraisal will be required. This is paid for by the lender.

Homes are required to be in good repair. Like both the HECM and Home Keeper, any items identified as in need of repair must be completed before closing, or the cost of the repairs will be escrowed and paid after they have been completed. Repairs must be completed within six months of the loan closing.

Account Types

The original Cash Account charged a 2-point origination fee and standard closing costs. A second and third loan option were added: the Zero Point and the Simply Zero loans. As you might be able to guess from their names, the Zero Point loan charges no points and the closing costs on the Simply Zero loan are simply zero.

Good Cents

One point is one percent of the total loan amount. A 2 percent origination fee on a $1,000,000 would be $20,000.

Standard Cash Account

The standard Cash Account has the highest closing costs and most flexible payment plan of the three account types. Closing costs are estimated as 2 percent of the principal loan amount as determined by the lender and has a scaled origination fee that is capped at 2 percent of the home's value.

The entire loan balance is placed in a credit line, which earns interest at a rate of 5 percent. This is a revolving line of credit, which you can draw and repay as you wish. If monthly payments are requested, these will be drawn and sent from the credit line.

You can pay any or all of the fees in cash at closing, or you can finance these as part of the loan.

Zero Point

The second account option is called Zero Point. With this option, you pay no origination fee. Standard third-party closing costs are charged (refer to Chapter 4 for a list of these). However, closing costs are limited to $3,500, excluding any state or local recording or transfer taxes.

Three quarters of the principal loan amount is required to be withdrawn at closing. The remaining quarter may be placed in a credit line and will earn interest at 5 percent until drawn.

There is no prepayment penalty on the loan if it is paid in full. Partial repayment of the amount drawn at closing is not allowed during the first five years.

Simply Zero

The newest addition to the product line is the Simply Zero loan. With this option, no closing costs or origination fees are charged, except any applicable state or local recording or transfer taxes. Costs are "simply zero."

The catch is that you must draw 100 percent of the principal loan amount as determined by the lender at closing. There is no prepayment penalty for full repayment, but no partial repayment is allowed for the first five years.

Using our example from the Typical Lump Sum Payments table, if the house is worth $1,000,000 and the couple is 82, the principal loan amount would be $352,600. The couple would be required to draw the full amount of $352,600, and this could not be repaid for the first five years.

Cash Account Versus HECM/Home Keeper

In the previous chapter on the Home Keeper, we compared the HECM and Home Keeper to see which would be a better choice in particular loan scenarios.

If you have a high-value home, more than $1,000,000, the Cash Account will yield the highest loan amount. However, *jumbo* refers to anything over the conforming limit as set by Fannie Mae. This is $359,650 for 2005. In some instances, the Cash Account loans may not be the best choice for higher-valued homes.

Talk the Talk _____

As you will recall from Chapters 4 and 5, Fannie Mae sets the conforming limit annually. For 2005, the conforming loan limit is $359,650. Any loan that is larger than this amount is called a **jumbo**.

If your home is close to $500,000 in terms of value, then the HECM and Home Keeper offer a cost-effective alternative. Let's look at our example of a 72-year-old borrower in Washington, D.C. We will assume a home value of $450,000, an expected average rate of 8 percent for the HECM, and that all closing costs are financed. So the loan amounts shown in the following table are the net amounts after closing costs have been deducted.

	HECM/ Mo.	Home Keeper	Simply Zero
Loan Amount	$138,878	$123,703	$132,885
Tenure	$1,087	$1,006	Not allowed
Closing Costs	$15,500	$10,700	$0

In this instance, even after financing $15,500 of closing costs, the HECM loan yields a higher payout to you.

The entire loan amount for the Simply Zero account must be drawn at closing. Interest will be charged on the entire balance for five years, at a rate that ranges 2 to 3 percent more than the HECM loan. The HECM and Home Keeper generally offer a better value for homes under $500,000.

The Least You Need to Know

- Cash Account loans are a better choice for homes valued at or near $1,000,000.
- Two Cash Account options offer lowered closing costs, but both require the borrower to draw a substantial portion of the loan at closing.

- A Cash Account also requires counseling.
- A Cash Account might not be the best choice for jumbo loans in the mid-500s price range.

Chapter 7

Applying for a Reverse Mortgage

In This Chapter

- Determining if your property is eligible
- Counseling requirements
- Choosing a loan and lender
- Preparing for the application

Which reverse mortgage program is the right one for you? And what kind of payment will work best? Your age, the type of property you own, the value of your home and your financial situation will probably narrow the choices for you.

This chapter walks you through the application process, and what you can expect along the way. First we explore what types of properties are eligible, then who has to get counseling, and how to choose a loan and a lender. Finally, we finish up with the application process and what paperwork you should have handy when you meet with the lender.

Eligible Properties

First, you must determine if your property is eligible for a reverse mortgage and which type it might qualify for.

Single-family, attached (townhouses, row houses, duplex, or twins) and detached houses, condominiums, and some manufactured homes are eligible for reverse mortgages. Multifamily dwellings, up to four-unit properties, are eligible if the borrower is living on the premises. Co-ops are not eligible for a reverse mortgage.

New construction is also not eligible. The house must be at least one year old, although there is no requirement about how long you have owned it.

Property requirements differ depending on the specific reverse mortgage you are interested in. For the FHA-insured HECM loan, properties must meet FHA guidelines. In broad terms, the property must be free of health and safety hazards and have no major structural defects. In practice, there is a laundry list of specific items that ensure this is the case (see Appendix C).

Co-ops and Condos

Co-ops are not eligible for a reverse mortgage, with one exception. One private company does reverse mortgages for million-dollar co-ops in New York City only. Other locations are being considered.

For both the HECM and the Home Keeper, the condominium must be "approved." A list of previously approved condominium projects is available on the HUD and Fannie Mae websites. Getting the entire project approved is expensive; so many condominiums are not on the list.

 Good Cents

The FHA condo approval list is available on the HUD website at https://entp. hud.gov/idapp/html/condlook.cfm. The Fannie Mae list of approved condos can be found at www.fanniemae.com.

If the condominium complex is not on the approved list, then the condominium units must be evaluated on a case-by-case basis. The management company must complete a *Spot Condo Approval* form, and they will often charge a small fee to do this. The completed form will be submitted to the lender for review. This will allow individual homeowners to gain approval for their unit only. This should be done early in the loan process to make sure your condominium qualifies before you spend the money to obtain an appraisal.

Talk the Talk

Spot Condo Approval—The general requirements for approval are at least 51 percent of the units must be owner-occupied; the condominium must have adequate financial reserves (savings) and no deferred maintenance (work that has been put off, perhaps because of lack of money). For the HECM loan, only 10 percent of the total loans in the complex can be FHA loans. The Home Keeper allows up to 20 percent of all loans in the complex to be Fannie Mae loans.

Unusual Properties

Mobile homes or "trailer" homes are generally parked on rented ground. These are considered to be personal property, not real estate, and are not eligible for a reverse mortgage.

Manufactured homes, on the other hand, may be. Manufactured homes must have been built after 1976, and must have a HUD-approved seal. These must be placed on an approved foundation and you must own the land on which they are placed. Additionally, manufactured homes must be in original condition, without any unusual "additions," such as add-on sunrooms or garages.

Log cabins and other "unusual" homes, including the house that grandpa built, may be eligible for government-insured loans if they meet HUD's Minimum Property Standards (MPS). A rule of thumb is if they will not meet local building codes, they probably will not meet HUD's MPS.

Working farms are considered commercial operations and are not eligible for a reverse mortgage. However, properties that were farms at one time, and are no longer working farms, may be eligible, as discussed in the "Excess Land" section. Out-buildings can still be in place, but they will not be valued for the purposes of the reverse mortgage.

Excess Land

In most cases, your home and land (up to five acres) are eligible for a reverse mortgage. If you own more than five acres, then the land must be subdivided into one lot that contains the house and five acres (for loan purposes) and the rest of the land. The rest of the land will not be considered for the purposes of the loan.

For example, if the house was sitting on a 20-acre parcel, then you might be required to subdivide the property into the house and five acres as one lot, and the remaining 15 acres as the second lot.

Legally subdividing the property can be expensive and time-consuming. In some areas it may be impossible, due to local restrictions.

If larger lots are typical to the area, then it may be acceptable to have the appraiser value the house with five acres separate from the rest of the property. However, then the excess land would be "tied up" in the mortgage. You could not sell excess land without repaying the mortgage.

Choosing the Loan

If you have a lower-priced home that needs repairs and are not looking for an additional source of income, then a single-purpose mortgage may be a good choice. Costs for this loan are lower and interest rates are generally very attractive. These loans have income requirements and are generally available only for low-income borrowers.

If you are seeking to pay off an existing mortgage or need an additional income source, the FHA-insured HECM loan may be an attractive alternative. The initial loan costs are higher, but this loan generally yields more cash than other options.

The yearly adjustable HECM has lower caps, limiting the potential that higher interest rates in the future will erode your equity. However, you pay for this option with a higher initial interest rate and lower lump sum or monthly payments up front.

The monthly adjustable option has higher caps and a lower interest rate to start. Therefore, borrowers get more money at the start of the loan.

Reverse mortgages are age-indexed, so older home-owners have access to a greater percentage of the equity in their homes than younger homeowners. Consequently, the "gap" between the monthly and yearly options closes as homeowners age.

The Home Keeper starts at a higher rate than the HECM loans, but will lend money for properties in areas where the FHA geographic limit is low, home values are higher, and borrowers are older, the cash available from this loan may be very close to the HECM.

If regular maintenance has not been done on a house, then it might need a number of small (or big) items repaired. FHA would require that all items be repaired, or that funds be escrowed to repair them. If there were enough small items, the sum might be more than the maximum repairs allowed by FHA. These might include a roof at the end of its economic life, missing railing, mixed polarity on the electric, broken windows, and non-working appliances.

The Home Keeper may also be used to purchase a home, and is the only loan designed to do that. So you can use equity from an existing home to buy a new one, and then live in it without a mortgage. This might be a nice option if you are downsizing, and moving closer to family.

Both the HECM and Home Keeper have lending limits. Homeowners with high-value homes will have access to a very small percentage of their

equity. The Cash Account is a clear winner in this situation, providing homeowners with the greatest access to equity. And although the initial interest is higher than the other two, the caps limit future interest rate growth to about the same as the HECM.

Review all the options before you make a choice. If working with an accountant or financial advisor, you should review the options with them to see which best meets your goals. It is a good idea to review the options with your family or executor, so they are aware of what you are trying to achieve.

Glance at the sample loan chart in Appendix B, which can give you an idea of what is available based on your age and home value. There are usually one or two good options, making the choice between loans fairly easy.

Counseling

All the reverse mortgage programs require counseling, which may be a meeting with a HUD-authorized representative or a telephone consultation with the representative's lender.

Counseling is provided free through HUD-trained counselors. It is preferred that counseling be done in person, but if this is not possible because of distance or health-related inability to get to a counselor, then counseling may be done over the phone. You will need to obtain counseling for the particular type of loan you wish to apply for. However,

if you are considering several, there is nothing forbidding you from going to more than one counseling session.

Make sure you tell your lender whether you have chosen telephone or face-to-face counseling. Either the counseling session or the loan application must be handled in person, so the lender needs to know this. The following sections discuss counseling in more detail.

Good Cents

If you are not sure what type of loan you are interested in, it may make sense to start with the lender first and figure out which is the best for your situation. The lender will, upon request, provide you with a list of counselors in your area. Note that lenders may not recommend any specific counselor or agency. This is known as "steering" and is not allowed by HUD.

Similarly, counselors are not allowed to "steer" customers to any particular lender either. They are required, if asked, to provide you with a list of lenders to choose from, and are not allowed to make any specific recommendations.

Counselors Protect You

Counseling is for your protection. A reverse mortgage is different from anything you've done before, and this will probably be the only reverse mortgage you ever take out. Therefore, you should get sound advice.

The loan officer can provide you with basic information about a loan, but they may handle only one type of loan. Because they are not accountants, financial planners, or lawyers, they cannot give you legal or financial planning advice.

Counselors are trained professionals, with backgrounds in debt counseling. Most are well informed about local loan programs and other types of aid that may be available to you. They are an unbiased third party with whom you can discuss your loan options as well as how these may fit into your lifestyle and budget.

Good Cents

Scheduling counseling can take a while. During peak times, it may take several weeks to get a counseling appointment set up. So plan to do this early in the process.

If you need counseling immediately (possible foreclosure, medical situation), tell the counseling agency that, and they will try to prioritize your appointment. If they cannot help you, call another counselor.

Who Must Receive Counseling

Everyone on the title to the property in question must receive counseling. So if you and a spouse jointly own the property, then both must receive counseling.

If a power of attorney (POA) will be signing the final documents, then both the homeowner and the POA must attend counseling. If the homeowner is unable to attend for medical reasons, then a doctor's letter to that effect may be required, and the POA may attend counseling instead of the homeowner.

An example of this would be a husband or wife whose spouse is incapable of handling his or her own affairs because of disease, such as Alzheimer's or dementia. In this case, the power of attorney must be in place, valid in the state, and must be "durable," meaning it must have specific language allowing the POA to continue if the person is incapacitated. If no power of attorney has been executed, then the able party would have to apply to the court for guardianship before applying for the loan.

If the property is in a *life estate*, all persons involved in the life estate must receive counseling: the borrower, beneficiaries, and trustees.

> **($) Talk the Talk** _____
>
> A **life estate** is a legal document that transfers title of the property to someone else, such as the homeowner's children, but grants the homeowner the right to use the property for their lifetime.

Adult children or anyone you choose may attend counseling with you, but only those on title are required to. Counseling can be done at that same time, or it can be done separately by each party. In most cases, counseling can be done in any state, not just the state where the property is located.

What the Counselor Does

There is certain basic information that a counselor must cover regarding the loan and how it works, but different agencies may provide different information. You will be required to provide a copy of your identifying documents (driver's license or picture ID, Social Security card, and so on).

Counselors may review your income and budget, your options, and the basic information about how the loan works. Most will request copies or information about your household bills. They may also request a copy of your deed and homeowner's insurance policy. They can make a recommendation or give you their opinion, but they do not have the authority to grant or deny a loan.

Counseling will generally take 45 minutes to an hour, depending on what questions you have. At the end of that period, the counselor will provide you with a certificate (generally two originals) indicating that you have completed this requirement.

The original counseling certificate must be signed by the borrower(s) and is valid for a period of 180 days. The lender will need an original certificate before they can proceed with the loan.

Choosing a Lender

If you have chosen a single-purpose or proprietary mortgage, you will be working with the lender or agency that administers those loans.

The HECM and Home Keeper products are strictly regulated, and the interest rates, margins, terms, and fees that may be charged are strictly regulated.

Initially 50 lenders were allowed to offer reverse mortgages, and this privilege was awarded by lottery. This is not the case anymore, but reverse mortgages are still a specialty product and not available from every bank or lender.

If you do counseling first, the counselor can provide you with a list of lenders. Or you may obtain a listing of lenders from the HUD website, from AARP, or through the National Reverse Mortgage Lenders Association.

Talk to several lenders and compare the programs they offer. Compare costs between lenders. Check with other people who have done a reverse mortgage and see who they used and how they felt about the experience. Find a loan officer you are comfortable working with. You will be working with this person for the next 30 to 60 days to process your loan.

What's Negotiable, What's Not

Rates and the FHA insurance premium are set and will vary between lenders for the HECM and Home Keeper. The monthly servicing fee is capped at $35 for the HECM monthly adjustment and $30 for the annual adjustment. Some lenders may charge less.

The origination fee may be negotiable. For house values under $100,000, a minimum fee will be charged and the lender probably will not negotiate at all. However, if you have a higher-priced property, they may be willing to pay for an appraisal or to cover some other costs as part of the deal.

Do not expect to get the origination fee cut in half, however. There are no hidden profits in reverse mortgages. Loan officers are often paid like real estate agents, where a portion of the origination fee is paid to the company they work for, and the balance is paid to them.

In addition, there are costs associated with the loan that the lender is not allowed to charge for. These

include underwriting or processing fees, and
courier fees to send documents back and forth.
These costs are paid from the origination fee.
What is left represents overhead and profit to the
lender and the loan officer. And let's be realistic,
nobody wants to work for free.

Initial Information

Initially, the loan officer will need some basic information to give you an accurate loan comparison.
They will ask for your personal information, including your name, address, zip code (very important), telephone number, birth date, the value of
your house, and if there are any outstanding liens.

They may also ask about your current financial
situation and what your goals are, so they can best
advise you.

Once you are ready to make an application, additional information will be required, and it will be
helpful to gather the documents you may need to
answer questions. Generally, an initial interview is
conducted over the phone, so correct paperwork
can be generated for your signature. The loan officer will need copies of these documents as well.

Documents Needed

In most cases, the first five documents on the following list are required by the loan officer when
you meet to sign an application. However, if you
have the documents together when you talk to

them on the phone, the loan officer can include the information in the typed loan documents. This will save time when you meet with him or her.

- Copy of your driver's license or other picture ID
- Copy of Social Security or Medicare card
- Copy of mortgage statement (if applicable) or name, address, telephone number, account number, and current balance
- Copy of declarations page of homeowner's insurance policy, or the contact information for the policy—name, address and telephone number of the agent, account number, annual premium, and if you know, the limits of coverage
- The original signed counseling certificate
- Copy of the original deed (helpful, but not required)
- Death certificate, if deceased spouse on title
- Copy of power of attorney, if this will be used
- Copy of trust or living will, if property is set up in either

What Information to Have at Hand

The loan officer will also ask for additional information about you and your property. You will also need to answer some questions to provide this information. The information and questions that might be asked of you include …

- An alternate contact name, address, and phone number, in case the lender is unable to contact you.

Good Cents

Before you call the loan officer, do a quick survey of your house so you are prepared to answer questions about the property.

- Do you have a wood stove, oil furnace or central air?
- Is this an urban or suburban home? Well and septic or city water and sewer? If well/septic, are city services available in your area?
- Are there any repairs required to the house at this time? Any visible peeling paint or water damage?
- What is the age of the house?
- What are houses in your neighborhood selling for?
- What type of property is it (detached, row house, condominium)? If the latter, what is the name and contact information for the management company?

- Do you have any outstanding debts or liens?
- Have you recently (past 10 years) been involved in a bankruptcy?
- Is there anyone else's name on the title?
- How big is your property (how much land)?

The more information you can provide at the beginning of the application process, the better. Potential problems can be resolved early in the loan process and will not hold up closing at the end.

After collecting the information, the loan officer will prepare the loan documents for signature. They will send these directly to you or meet with you to review them, as agreed between you.

The loan package will be about 30 pages in length, including the actual application and all pertinent disclosures. This varies from state to state. In addition, the loan officer is required to provide you with a copy of the sample mortgage note and printed materials as detailed in the loan disclosures. These change from time to time, but include information about closing costs, variable rate loans, and the reverse mortgage.

The loan officer will collect copies of the documents and the original counseling certificate. They will generally leave an unsigned copy of all the loan documents you signed.

If the lender charges an application fee, then they will collect this at that time. This will typically cover the cost of the appraisal fee and other third-party charges. If not, the loan officer should tell you what comes next and what costs you can expect to pay out-of-pocket. This is generally the appraisal cost and any required inspections.

The Least You Need to Know

- Everyone on title to the property must receive counseling.
- Excess land may be handled through the appraisal, or the land may have to be legally subdivided.
- If you are not sure what type of loan you want, start with the loan officer first.
- Gather contact information, including zip codes and account numbers, and make copies of necessary documents.

Chapter 8

The Approval Process

In This Chapter

- What happens once you've signed papers
- What hiccups you can expect in the process
- What your rights as a borrower are

You've been to counseling, chosen the type of loan, and picked out a lender to work with. You've met with the lender's representative, and signed a lot of papers. So what happens now?

What happens next is the approval process, which is the subject of this chapter. You get a peek into the lender's side of the loan process. The appraisal and required inspections must be done, a title search is ordered and checked, and assuming there are no issues, closing is set up to finalize the loan.

What Happens Now (the Approval Process)

After the lender has the signed loan documents *and* the counseling certificate, they go to work. They will check the mailing address for the property, generally with the post office. In some rural areas, properties are identified as only a lot and block and have no actual address. In this case, the appraiser will be instructed to check this when they make their property review.

For an HECM loan, a credit report will be requested. If state or federal tax liens are present, these will be required to be paid at closing.

Good Cents

If you think there might be an issue with your credit, such as a judgment or lien that has not been paid, then you might want to request a credit report before applying for a loan. If you have already paid off the problem loan and have paperwork to show that, you should make a copy of this for the loan officer.

If you do not expect any problems, then I would not worry about getting a credit report beforehand. The loan officer will give you a copy of it when they receive it. No sense in paying for it twice.

The lender will request an FHA case number. For government-insured loans, this will act as a tracking number. In order to get the case number, the lender will have to verify the address for FHA, assign an appraiser, and verify your correct name and Social Security number.

Your personal information will be checked through CAIVRS, the Credit Alert Interactive Voice Response System. This is a system developed by HUD to allow federal agencies to check for any outstanding federal debt, including unpaid student loans. If there is, it may invalidate the loan, but often an outstanding balance can be paid at closing.

Once this is complete, any required inspections will be ordered. These include the appraisal and termite inspection. If problems or special conditions are identified in the appraisal, other inspections may be required.

The cost of these inspections is your responsibility. In most cases, the cost will be collected when the inspection is done. In some cases, the company may bill the lender, and this will be collected at closing.

 Good Cents _____

You have the right to cancel the loan at any point in time, and for any reason. However, if you do cancel the loan, you will still be responsible for any third-party charges—namely the inspections done for your home.

The Appraisal

The appraisal is an independent valuation of your home's value, as determined by a licensed, trained third party. The appraisal is the key to the loan transaction, because it is the security for the loan. (This will be discussed in more detail in Chapter 9.)

The appraisal cost is considered a "third-party" charge. The cost may be included in the lender's application fee. If the lender does not collect an application fee, you will probably be asked to "pay at the door" or when the appraiser makes the inspection visit. If the fee is to be collected at closing and you elect not to continue with the loan, this fee will still be owed.

Generally, the appraisal will be delivered to the lender within five business days of the inspection visit. The value will be determined by the appraisal, and it will also identify any conditions that might be an issue. The FHA appraisal contains a "Notice to Homebuyer" which details the conditions for the loan, which must be signed and returned to the lender.

Good Cents

If you have an issue with the appraisal, because of a low value or a condition that you do not think is warranted, you have the option to request a field review.

The loan officer will send the appraisal to another appraiser for review. If they agree with the original appraiser, then you agree to accept the appraisal. If they disagree, they will request that the original appraiser prove his work, and generally the appraisal will be adjusted.

There is a fee for this service, probably $250–$300. Ask the loan officer before you order this. Do not order a second appraisal. The lower of the two values will be used, which is probably the appraisal you already have.

Inspections

A termite inspection is required for all properties, except condominiums. If a problem item is noted in the appraisal, other inspections may be required. And there are some specific items that will always require an inspection.

Termite Inspection

All single-family properties must be inspected for termite infestations. As the termite inspection is good for only 90 days, this will generally not be ordered until after the appraisal has been received. The inspection is to verify that there is no current termite infestation at the property.

If there is any visible damage to the house, such as settlement of bricks, missing mortar from fireplaces, or water damage, then an inspection of the condition by a licensed contractor may be required. In addition, there are some specific items that will always require an inspection.

Woodstove

If you have a woodstove, then you will need a certification that the woodstove has been properly installed. In some areas, the local fire department or building inspector may be able to certify this—at no cost or for a small donation (to fire department). In most areas, you will need to get a woodstove/fireplace company to prepare this. They will generally charge a fee of $50 to $100.

If you are having other work or estimates prepared, you may be able to get the general contractor doing the estimates to prepare the certification. It doesn't cost anything to ask, and the general contractor may just do it for free because he or she will be doing other work at the house.

Well/Septic Systems

Well systems will need to be tested for bacteria, lead, iron, nitrates, sand, and turbidity (how clear the water is). The water testing may be done by a water company, or you can save some money and do this yourself. Generally testing companies will send you the sample collection bottle and instructions, and this must be collected and sent by overnight mail to the lab. Testing generally takes 24 hours.

If the water test indicates a problem, then you will have to have the well treated to correct this. In most cases, this must be done prior to loan closing. In some cases, such as sand in the water, the problem can be corrected by installing a water filtration system. This might be included in "required repairs," which will be discussed in Chapter 9.

If the appraiser indicates that there might be a problem with the septic system, then this will have to be inspected as well. Generally, however, the lender will simply require that the location of the septic, well, and drain fields are shown on the appraisal.

Roofs

The appraiser will make an inspection of the roof and attic to look for signs of water damage and leaking. Shingled roofs should have a remaining life of at least two years. If not, or if the condition cannot be determined due to weather conditions such as snow, then the appraiser will recommend a roof inspection.

Good Cents _____

If you have a copy of your house location survey, this should show the location of the well, septic, and drain fields. This was probably done when you bought the house, and is a drawing by a survey which shows the property boundaries, the house, and all structures on the property. This document would be sufficient to show the appraiser or lender the dimensions and location of the well/septic.

In some cases, the lender will accept the homeowner's sketch and certification of the location of the well/septic, if all else fails.

All single-family units and small multifamily units with a flat roof require a roof inspection.

The cost of any additional inspections and the cost for estimates is the responsibility of the home-owner.

Title Search

A title search is a review of the ownership of the property over a period of years. Typically, a title company will send someone to the courthouse to obtain a copy of the original deed for the property and will trace the ownership of the property and look for any outstanding judgments or liens.

One of the most frequent problems uncovered is an unreleased trust. This would be a mortgage that may have been paid off some time in the past but which has not been "released" at the courthouse, so it is still showing up on the title.

In this case, the lender will contact you for assistance to prove that the loan has been paid. Ideally, they will be able to get a "Certificate of Satisfaction" from the previous lender. This is a legal document that can be recorded at the courthouse stating the loan had been satisfied, or paid in full.

Other items that may be helpful to prove the loan has been paid are a "Paid in Full" letter from the previous lender. If the loan was paid off during a refinance, then a copy of the settlement paperwork showing the payoff may be helpful.

The most common occurrence of unreleased loans is for home equity loans. These are hybrid loans, a flexible line of credit that can be used like a credit card, and are relatively new to the industry. Lines of credit that are paid off may be closed, but not released from the title.

A second common issue is a deceased spouse listed on the title. This can be addressed easily by providing a copy of the death certificate for the deceased spouse. An original copy will be required prior to closing.

Liens for taxes and unpaid contractor's work may also be on title. Tax liens are the only liens that can take precedence over a mortgage, and these will be required to be paid prior to, or at, closing.

Simply put, the state or IRS can force the sale of a property to collect unpaid taxes, and they will collect their money first. Any other creditor (lender) will be paid after the government gets its money. So the lender will require that these be paid current, and kept current, during the life of the loan.

Insurance

Homeowner's insurance is required for every loan. This guarantees that, if the house is damaged or destroyed, money will available to repair or replace the dwelling. In the event of a total loss, it guarantees that the insured party will be reimbursed for their losses.

The lender will require that the value of the loan be insured. If the appraised value of the house is $250,000, then the replacement cost for the insurance must be $250,000.

Sounds simple, but in some urban areas where land value is very high, this can be problematic. Insurance companies base their insured value on replacement cost only. If it costs $100,000 to rebuild a house, and the appraised value of the dwelling is $250,000, then the insurance company may be unwilling to insure the higher amount.

The lender will not give you a loan on an underinsured property, as they will not be repaid if the property is destroyed. The only solution in this instance is to change insurance companies if you want the loan.

Closing

Once all the conditions have been met, inspections done, and estimates (if any) collected, then the loan should be approved and you are ready for closing.

The lender will contact you a few days before closing to make sure how you want payments to be distributed. At this point, you must decide if you want money at closing, money in a credit line, or monthly payments, and how much.

The lender will schedule a closing date and time that is mutually convenient. Depending on the lender and state regulations, you may have to go to a settlement agent's office or a notary may be sent to your home with paperwork for your signature.

Rest your hand for a day or so before closing. Typically, the "closing package" will consist of three or more original copies of all documents, which all will have to be signed. This will be 100 pages or more, with all the state, federal, and lender disclosures making up the bulk of the package.

The "important" paperwork is the settlement statement, which details the costs associated with the loan and the cash generated to you. This is really the heart of the loan transaction and should be explained in detail. It should be close to the Good Faith Estimate that you were originally given by the lender, and any deviation from the estimated amounts should be clear and explained.

Costs that are based on a percentage of your loan amount will vary. These costs include the title insurance and state and county recording taxes.

The cash available to you is based on the value of your home and the interest rate at closing. Any estimated repairs will be deducted from the cash available to you.

As with the original loan documents, a complete copy of all documents you are asked to sign will be given to you at closing. You don't have time to read through these at closing, but do make a point of reviewing the important information over the next few days.

All residential loans have a three-day right of rescission period. For up to three days after the loan is closed, you may cancel the loan for any reason. Maybe you won the lottery, changed your mind, or the loan did not provide as much money as you expected, because of interest rate changes, because of the value of the house, or because there were more repairs required than expected. It doesn't matter why.

After the rescission period has passed, the loan will be "funded." At this point, any outstanding liens will be paid, such as overdue tax liens and any current mortgage balance. If you have requested cash at closing, then this check will be deposited in your bank or a check sent directly to you, as you have requested.

If you think you may have an immediate need for cash, it is a good idea to request that amount at closing. It generally takes 30 to 45 days for your account to be set up with the lender, and it will be that long before you can access your credit line or expect your first monthly payment, whichever you specified.

If there are any problems with the paperwork, such as missing signatures or incorrect information, then the lender will request that you sign some portion of the documents again. Typically, funding will be delayed for several days until the error has been corrected.

The Least You Need to Know

- The costs for the appraisal, termite, and any other required inspections are your responsibility. These will have to be paid even if you cancel the loan.
- Other inspections may be required if the appraiser identifies a problem.
- Title issues often hold up approval.
- If repairs are required, you will need to get the work done, or get an estimate for the work.
- You may cancel the loan for any reason, before, during or up to three days after settlement. This is called the rescission period, and the loan will not be funded until this has expired.

Chapter 9

The Property Appraisal

In This Chapter

- The purpose of the appraisal
- How value is determined
- What you can do to increase value

The property appraisal is key to the loan transaction because the property is the "security" for the loan. The property's value and any required repairs will be established by the appraisal. And the property must meet a set of minimum standards in order to be eligible for a reverse mortgage.

In this chapter, we explore the three approaches to value used by appraisers, conditions that might cause a problem, how repairs will be handled, and what you can do to prepare for the appraiser's visit.

The Appraisal

The purpose of an appraisal is to determine the property's fair market value. This is the value that the homeowner would *most likely* receive if they were to sell the property today. Note that this is not the asking price or sale price, and it probably is not the highest value that the homeowner might get, but the most likely price a buyer might pay for the property.

Appraisers use three different methods to determine value: sales comparison, reconstruction cost, and income approach. The sales comparison approach assumes that a buyer will pay about the same price for a similar property. The appraiser locates comparable properties, similar in design, size, and location. He usually chooses three or four to compare the house's value to. Adjustments are made to account for differences in size, amenities, and date of sale. A simple version of the formula the appraiser uses is shown in the following:

> Sales Price of Comp +/– Adjustments = Adjusted Value

The cost approach assumes that a savvy shopper would not pay more than it costs to rebuild the house on a similar property. The property's value is *depreciated*, or adjusted, by its remaining useful life. For example, if a house cost $180,000 to rebuild and it has suffered normal "wear and tear" for a few years, depreciation might be 10 percent:

> Rebuild Cost – Depreciation + Land Value = Property Value
>
> $180,000 – (10% x 180,000) + $75,000 = $237,000

> **$** **Talk the Talk**
>
> **Depreciation** is the loss of use or loss of value due to physical deterioration—in other words, wear and tear—or functional or external obsolescence. Functional obsolescence could be an outdated floor plan or inadequate mechanical system. External obsolescence would be changes in outside factors, like rezoning of the neighborhood to commercial or increased traffic noise due to a change in traffic patterns. All of these items may decrease the value of a property.

The income approach is generally used for multi-family houses, which may be collecting rental income. In this case, the unit would be compared to other properties in the area to determine the "market rent" or average rent that other units may obtain. The value of the property is adjusted for the amount of rent that is collected.

Typically, the sales comparison carries the most weight and is accepted as the market value. The cost approach is also calculated and usually supports this value.

Good Cents

Although you pay for the appraisal, it "belongs" to the lender, and you must request a copy of it in writing. This is to prevent the possibility of fraud, where a homeowner would alter the appraisal to suit their own purposes. An appraisal must be delivered from the appraiser to the lender directly.

FHA appraisers view the property with a more critical eye. They are required to check a "representative sampling" of outlets and light fixtures, check for leaks, water flow, and obvious safety issues, to name just a few.

Newer homes generally qualify, but older homes often need a few "tweaks" to meet FHA guidelines. Some of the most common items identified in older homes are ...

- Lack of GFI outlets in bathroom. These are special electrical outlets with a built-in circuit breaker that will turn off if an electrical appliance (such as a hair dryer) falls into water.

- Lack of handrails on exterior stairs. If there are three or more steps outside the house, a handrail is required. There are no specific requirements as to height or materials, just that it be in place and is sturdy.

- Peeling paint. Any surfaces that have peeling paint, inside or out, must be scraped and repainted.

- Smoke detectors. Always a good idea, smoke detectors must be installed to meet local building codes.

None of these "defects" is difficult or expensive to resolve. These can be corrected prior to the loan, or an estimated amount can be "escrowed" (held by the lender in a separate account) to do the repairs at a later time.

Some of the guidelines may be more difficult to work around, and may be deal killers. These are ...

- No wood to earth contact. The wooden foundation may not be in contact with the ground. There must be six inches between the ground and wood beam of the foundation.

- Potential falling tower. If there is a tower visible from the house (for example, power lines) and there is the possibility that if it falls it might hit the house, then the loan cannot be insured by FHA.

- Water/sewer hookups. If a property is on a well or septic and county/city water or sewer hookups are available, then the property must connect to these.

A standard appraisal is required for the Home Keeper. An FHA appraisal is required for the Cash Account. Requirements for a standard appraisal are less specific than for an FHA appraisal. Again, in broad terms, the property must be free from obvious defects or structural problems. And for homes over $1 million in value, two appraisals often are required to establish the value.

Required Repairs

If "repairs" to the property are identified on the appraisal or in subsequent inspections that were requested by the appraiser, then they must be completed to get the reverse mortgage. Repairs may be handled one of two ways. You can have the items repaired before the mortgage is completed. The repairs must be checked by the appraiser, who will charge a small fee for the return visit.

If required repairs are less than $500, the lender will require that these be completed and re-inspected before closing on the loan.

The other option is to obtain estimates for the repair work. For small repairs, the lender will escrow as much as three times the cost of the repairs. For larger amounts, they will escrow up to 1.5 times the estimated amount. A small fee is charged for administration of the repair funds. These amounts will be withheld from the loan funds.

15 Percent Restriction

If the required repairs exceed 15 percent of the loan amount, then the property will not be eligible for a reverse mortgage. If this is the situation, some repairs can be made (to bring the amount of the repairs down below the 15 percent limit). The property must be re-inspected by the appraiser to certify the repairs were completed satisfactorily.

If the required repairs exceed 30 percent of the loan amount, then the property is not eligible for the reverse mortgage at all. In most cases, the property will be in "fair" condition or so run down that it needs a total overhaul to be habitable.

How Repairs Are Handled

After the loan closing, you may have the repairs done, pay for them, and submit the receipts to the lender for review. The appraiser will be sent out to check the repairs, for which they will charge a small fee. Once approved, the amount for the repairs as well as any excess money will be re-funded to you.

If repairs are costly, a deposit and progress payments can be arranged with the lender. However, the lender may require that the progress be checked by the appraiser along the way, and they will charge a fee for each visit.

Good Cents

A fee is charged monthly to keep track of the repair funds. So it makes sense to have repairs done quickly to minimize your costs.

Preparing for an Appraisal

Although the appraiser is not interested in your housekeeping skills, color choices, or design sense, a clean house "shows" better than a dirty one. First impressions count, and you want to get the top "market" value for your house. So do the following to prepare for the appraisal …

- Clean, clean, and clean. Clean dirty hand-prints from doors, halls, and walls. Vacuum the carpet and mop the kitchen floor.

- Clear away clutter and make sure the appraiser has easy access in every room.

- Turn on the heater and the air conditioning to make sure these are in good working order—blowing hot air and cold air, as appropriate.

- Check electrical outlets to make sure they work, and replace any burnt out bulbs, so visibility is not an issue.

- If there is an attic or crawl space, make sure the way is clear and the bulbs in those areas are working.

- Scrape and repaint areas that have peeling paint, inside and out. This is particularly common on outside windows and sills, decks, and porches.

- Repair any dripping or leaking faucets or fixtures. Clean any water stains.

- Repair holes in flooring or walls. Look for "tripping hazards" and make sure these are repaired.

- Clean and trim the yard. Dispose of any debris or old junk, tires, and so on, that is lying around.

Use common sense. You don't need a total rehabilitation of the house, but these are small things you can do to improve the value of your home, and consequently increase the amount of your loan, too.

And last but not least, be nice to the appraiser. It is not supposed to matter, but in the real world, appraisal values do tend to be slightly higher when the appraiser likes the house and homeowner. If you argue with or are rude to your appraiser, it could end up costing you money.

The Least You Need to Know

- The appraisal is the key to the reverse mortgage, because the house is the security for the loan.

- A property on well and septic that can connect to city water and sewer will be required to do so.

- Peeling paint on the exterior is one of the most common items noted for repair on an appraisal.

- Make your house as inviting as possible. First impressions count.

Living with a Reverse Mortgage

In This Chapter

- How to manage repair escrows
- Your rights and responsibilities
- Loan repayment
- What are your payments and other benefits

You've closed on your loan. Congratulations.

Now it's time to turn your attention to what life is like after closing.

Repair Escrows

If you were required to make repairs and chose to do them after closing, then the lender will have collected the costs of the repairs plus a cushion. The cushion can be up to 3 percent for small costs and 1.5 percent for larger repairs.

Within several weeks, you will receive a welcoming package from the lender. This will include information about who to contact to schedule repairs and where to send invoices. Call your contact person with any questions.

Good Cents _____

> If repairs are large, then you can coordinate the repairs and payment through the lender. If they are small or you would prefer to do them yourself, go ahead. Keep your receipts to send to the lender when the work is done. They will send the appraiser to inspect, and then release the balance of the escrowed funds.

Schedule the repairs as quickly as possible. The lender will charge a small monthly fee for the administration of the repair funds. So you need to get this done quickly.

Once repairs have been completed, the lender will request that the appraiser revisit the property to certify the repairs are completed. The appraiser will sign off on the repairs, and only then will the lender release the funds. Unless you have made the repairs yourself, a check typically will be sent jointly to you and the contractor, and both signatures will be required before it can be deposited.

Good Cents

Make sure your contractor is aware that you are working with an escrow fund. Otherwise, they will expect to be paid when the job is completed, rather than after it has been inspected. This typically delays payment 5 to 10 days, and will irritate the contractor if he is not expecting to wait for his money.

Once all repairs are made, certified by the appraiser and paid, the balance in the repair fund will be released to you.

Paying Taxes and Insurance

You are required to pay state and local property taxes annually. You are also required to have a homeowner's insurance policy, and to keep it current, to protect your home against damage by fire, storms, or freak accidents like falling trees. These items are covered under standard homeowner's policies.

If you have had a mortgage on your home, then the lender probably collected and paid both the taxes and the homeowner's insurance on your behalf. If you wish to continue paying them this way, contact your lender and see if they will do this. Some will and some won't.

Good Cents _____

> If your home is located within a flood plain, the lender will notify you and you will be required to have special flood insurance. Generally these are properties around bodies of water, so you probably would already be aware of this. Flooding is not covered under standard home-owner's policies. Shop around. Rates for flood insurance vary quite a bit.

If you have a line of credit and the lender allows it, the tax and insurance costs may be deducted and paid annually. If you have tenure or term payments, the lender can collect one twelfth of the costs each month and pay them when due.

Use Caution _____

> Property taxes must be paid in a timely manner. The lender has the right to suspend any payments to you until they are paid. If you've taken a lump sum and refuse to pay taxes, the lender can demand payment in full for the loan.
>
> Tax liens are one of the few things that take precedence over a loan—or the taxman gets his money before your lender. So they don't want taxes to be past due.

If you have been paying your taxes and insurance yourself, you can continue to do so. Some local governments offer a discounted rate if taxes are paid early. Insurance companies will typically accept payments on a monthly basis, but generally offer a better rate if the insurance is paid annually. Take advantage of these discounts if you are paying on your own and you can afford to make the lump payments.

Maintaining Your Property

Routine maintenance will save you time and money by preventing significant repairs for untreated damage. As a reverse mortgage borrower, you are required to keep your home in the same condition it was when the loan was made. Likely you would do this anyway, to keep your home looking good. A checklist of items is often a handy reminder. The following lists outline maintenance activities you should perform seasonably:

In the Spring:

- Service air conditioner
- Take down storm windows and replace screens
- Clean fireplace or woodstove
- Check weather stripping and replace if necessary
- Check basement for dampness
- Check/clean dryer vent and exhaust fans

- Check/repair peeling or chipped paint
- Check/repair damaged caulking
- Check/repoint brick/block
- Drain hot water heater and clear sediment

 Good Cents _____

> You can save money by having work done early in the spring for air-conditioning service, fireplace cleaning, and repair work. This is the lean season for most contractors, and they will often "cut you a break" in order to get work done early in the season.

In the Fall:

- Clear gutters of leaves and debris
- Service furnace and change filters
- Check insulation and window/door weather stripping, and repair as necessary
- Drain outside faucets
- Clean/store screens and replace storm windows/doors
- Check for cracks/holes in siding/foundation and fill holes
- Check roof for leaks

- Remove window air conditioners and store
- Check chimney for obstructions, and make sure damper closes completely

Good Cents

You may find it cost effective to switch some of the routine tasks and save money. For instance, chimney sweepers get a lot of calls in the fall as people begin to use their fireplaces. Furnace maintenance companies are also busy in the fall. Call in the spring instead.

The Complete Idiot's Guide for Handling Household Disasters details how to handle small repairs and problems you may encounter with maintenance. This might be a good investment if you are not familiar with how to fix the drips, leaks, and other minor disasters that seem to crop up from time to time.

Certifying Your Occupancy

The reverse mortgage loan requires that you occupy your home as your permanent residence. The lender may occasionally contact you by phone or by mail to verify this fact. So if you are planning an extended vacation (two months or more), you should notify the lender and give them an alternate contact.

Repaying the Loan

The loan becomes due when you sell your home or transfer title to someone else, when the last surviving borrower dies, or when you cease to live in the house as your primary residence. It may also become due if you fail to meet your responsibilities: maintaining the home as your primary residence, keeping the house in good repair, and paying both insurance and property taxes in a timely manner.

The loan balance is generally paid off from the sale of the home, but this is not required. The loan can be paid from proceeds of a life insurance policy or from a conventional loan, if the family wishes to keep the home. If the family wishes to keep the home but cannot pay off the loan, then the house will have to be sold.

No Prepayment Penalty

The reverse mortgages have no prepayment penalties, so you can pay the loan off in full at any time.

Partial vs. Full Repayment

You can make partial payments on all loans except the Cash Account, which prohibits partial prepayment of the amount "drawn" at closing for the first five years. Credit lines are "revolving" and can be drawn from and paid at any time. However, if you pay the entire loan balance, then the loan is automatically closed.

If you itemize tax deductions and have sufficient income to make additional interest payments, then you might want to pay some of the interest you are being charged. The interest is deductible only if it is paid during the calendar year you are filing taxes. Talk to your accountant or financial advisor about whether this would be beneficial for you.

If you wanted to keep the loan balance small, you might also want to make partial payments. Find out when the bank credits funds received. Many only "credit" these once a month, so you will want to have money received by the date when the funds are received.

How Much Will You Owe?

It will take several weeks after closing before you will receive a welcome package from the lender, although sometimes this is given out at closing. This should contain basic information about the loan, including who to call and instruction for changing your payment plan, repair escrows, and so on.

If you have chosen the HECM loan, you will receive monthly statements regarding the loan activity and interest rate changes and charges. The lender is required to send you an annual statement detailing the loan activity during the year as well.

If you have chosen the Home Keeper loan, the lender is required to send quarterly statements regarding loan activity and interest charges for the previous three months.

If you want to change payment plans, this would be a good time to do it while you have all the information in hand. The lender will charge a small fee, which will be added to the loan balance.

Review statements carefully. The current interest rate for the loan, the payments made to date, and the balance owed will be listed in this statement. This will be your most accurate source of information regarding the loan.

The Least You Need to Know

- You can do repairs yourself, or have a contractor do them. Repairs must be inspected by the appraiser before funds will be released.

- The lender may charge a monthly fee for managing escrow money. So get repairs done quickly to save yourself money.

- You can make partial repayments on the loan at any time, but if you pay it in full the loan will be automatically closed.

- Property taxes and insurance must be paid. Failure to do so could cause your loan to be in default.

Glossary

annuity   Generally involves a contract sold by an insurance company and a capital investment that provides minimum payments over a specific period of time. Payments are typically made after retirement and the investment is tax-deferred.

appraisal   An evaluation of property by a trained, independent third party.

ARM   Adjustable Rate Mortgage. The interest rate on a loan. The rate for the loan may change.

CAIVRS   Credit Alert Interactive Voice Response System. A credit check system developed by HUD for use by all federal agencies to check for any federal debt owed.

cap   The maximum interest rate that can be charged on a loan.

depreciation   An adjustment made for loss of use of a product because of physical age, damage, or obsolescence (outdated or unusable).

DPL   Deferred Payment Loan. Loan on which payments are not required until some later date, as determined by the loan terms.

equity   The difference between the value of real estate and any loans secured by the real estate.

escrow   Money held by the lender for the benefit of the homeowner. Typically, funds for the cost of repairs may be held in escrow.

FHA   Federal Housing Administration, a division of HUD (Housing and Urban Development), is responsible for administering the government home loan insurance program.

FNMA   Fannie Mae, a quasi-government agency created in the 1930s to promote a secondary market for mortgages.

HECM   Home Equity Conversion Mortgage. An FHA-insured reverse mortgage.

Home Keeper   Fannie Mae's proprietary reverse mortgage.

house location survey   A scaled drawing of a property showing the property boundaries and the location of any structures on the property, such as house, shed, garage, and fence.

HUD   U.S. Department of Housing and Urban Development. HUD's mission is to increase home-ownership and affordable housing.

index   A published rate that represents the value of the securities that make it up, such as the 1-year Treasury bill rate.

lien   A loan or judgment that must be cleared before the property can be sold.

margin   Fixed amount added to an index to determine what the current interest charge will be.

MIP   Mortgage Insurance Premium. MIP is the insurance paid by a homeowner to ensure the lender against losses.

mortgage   A loan that is secured by real estate.

non-recourse loan   A loan secured by real estate. The real estate cannot be sold or disposed of without paying off the loan, and the real estate is the only asset that may be used to repay the loan.

plat   *See* "House Location Survey."

prepayment penalty   A penalty for paying off a mortgage before it is due.

reverse annuity mortgage   A reverse mortgage with a limited term, usually 10 years, which pays a fixed amount per month as income.

servicing fee   Monthly fee charged by the lender for administering your account.

service set-aside   This sum is the value of the monthly servicing fee over the life of the loan.

title   A document that shows who is the owner of the home.

variable rate   A rate that can change over the life of the loan. Variable rate is generally calculated as the following: Index + Margin = Interest Rate.

viager   *En viager* means "for life." Viager is a private variation of reverse mortgage popular in France.

Loan Type Comparison: HECM, Home Keeper, and Private

The following chart is a quick comparison between the three major reverse mortgage programs.

	HECM	Home Keeper	Cash Account
Max Limit 2005	$312,896 (depends on area)	$359,650	No maximum limit
Loan Amount Based on -	Home Value or Max Claim Limit	Home Value or lending limit	Home Value, No limit
	Age of Borrower	Age & # borrowers	Age & # borrowers
	Expected int. rate	Int. rate affects calculation	Int. rate affects calculation
Eligible Properties	Single-family, 1–4 unit, Condos, PUDs, Manufactured Homes	Single-family, 1–4 unit, Condos, PUDs, No Manufactured Homes	Single family, 1–4 unit, Condos, PUDs, Manufactured Homes Co-ops, NY only
Interest Rate	1-year T-bill	1-month CD index	6-month Libor
Margin	1.5% Monthly/3.1% Annual	3.4%	5%

	HECM	Home Keeper	Cash Account
Caps Start rate +	10% for Monthly/ 5% for Annual	12%	6%
Fees			
Origination Fee	$2,000 or 2%	$,2000 or 2%	Depends on product
Mortgage Insurance	2% of Max Claim	No MIP	No MIP
Closing Cost	Allowed 3rd party Charges	Allowed 3rd party Charges	Depends on product
Payment Plans	Tenure	Tenure	Depends on product
	Term	Line of Credit	Line of Credit
	Line of Credit	Modified Tenure	Partial or full draw
	Modified Tenure		at closing
	Modified Term		

continues

continued

	HECM	Home Keeper	Cash Account
Credit Line	Earns Interest. Current Rate + 5%	No Interest	Depends on product. 5% on Standard
Service Fee	Yes	Yes	Yes, except IL & MD
Prepayment Penalty	None	None	None for full. Restricted 5 years depending on product.
Appraisal	FHA Appraisal	"As Is" Appraisal	FHA Appraiser "as is." 2nd appraisal if over $2,000,000 value

Sample Loan Comparison (Costs/Yields)

The following chart is similar to the comparison you will receive when you make an application for a reverse mortgage. It compares several different plans so you can judge which might be the most beneficial for you.

	FHA Monthly	FHA Yearly	Home Keeper
Initial Rate	6.41%	8.01%	8.06%
Expected Rate	8.0%	9.6%	8.06%
Rate Cap	16.41%	13.01%	20.06%
Home Value	$225,000	$225,000	$225,000
Credit Line Rate	6.91%	8.51%	0
Principal Limit	$114,300	$91,125	$86,796
Set-aside	–$4,471	–$3,357	–$3,690
Available Principal Limit	$109,829	$87,768	$83,106
MIP	–$4,500	–$4,500	–$0
Orig. Fee	–$4,500	–$4,500	–$4,500
Closing	–$2,500	–$2,500	–$2,500
Net Principal Limit	$98,329	$76,268	$76,106
Tenure Payments	$770	$682	$619

FHA Property Guidelines

This appendix provides a quick reference to FHA Property Guidelines. For more complete information, refer to the HUD Handbook 4510.2, which can be viewed or downloaded from the HUD website at www.hud.gov. Follow the Resources link to Handbooks.

The FHA property standards require that the property, including the heating, electric, mechanical, plumbing, and structural systems of the house, should be safe, sanitary, and in good repair.

In theory, that doesn't sound too bad. However, the FHA property standards are quite specific about what they consider safe, sanitary, and in good repair to be. The following lists provide a bit more explanation and some specific examples you might find useful.

Exterior

- **Roof.** The roof should be watertight and in good repair, with a remaining physical life of at least two years. Evidence of worn, damaged, or missing shingles requires inspection. A flat roof requires inspection, unless it is a shared roof, such as the roof on a condominium that covers multiple units.

- **Siding.** Siding should be in good condition with no missing or damaged portions.

- **Foundation.** A six-inch clearance must exist between a wood foundation and earth. The foundation may be covered by siding as long as it is not wood.

- **Gutter/Downspout.** Must be installed if roof overhang is less than 12 inches. Gutter and downspouts must be in good repair.

- **Crawl Space.** Must have an 18-inch clearance, be clear of debris, appear dry, and have a passable service door.

- **Basement.** Must be dry and have no observable structural problems.

- **Brick/Block.** Mortar between brick and block must be in good condition. Tuck-pointing is required if deteriorated mortar is visible.

- **Handrail.** All exterior stairs with more than three steps require a handrail.

- **Paint.** Any surfaces, inside or out, with peeling paint must be scraped and repainted.

- **Private Roads.** Private roads must have a private road agreement that addresses maintenance and access.

- **Well/Septic.** Certification of water from the well is required to meet FHA requirements for contaminants. Shared wells require a Shared Well Agreement.

The septic must be in good condition with no visible problems. The well must be a minimum of 15 feet from the house and 10 feet from the property line. The well must be 50 feet from the septic tank and 100 feet from the drain field.

- **Pest Inspection.** A termite inspection is required in most areas.

Interior

- **Plumbing.** Water flow must be adequate, with no visible evidence of water damage or deterioration to pipes and fixtures.

- **Heating.** Furnaces must be in good repair and provide adequate heat (at least 50 degrees). Wall-mounted heaters must be permanently affixed and adequately vented. Older furnaces require certification.

- **Wood Stoves.** Must be permanently installed, not just left loose in place, and installation must be inspected for adherence to building and fire code regulations. For example, it must be 3' or more from any flammable surface.

- **Electric.** Knob and tube electric systems require certification for safety. 60-Amp service may be acceptable if it provides adequate power (approx. 1,100 square feet with no central air-conditioning). 100-Amp service is preferred. Kitchens and bathrooms must have three-prong ground outlets.

- **Appliances.** Should be in good repair and in operable condition.
- **Walls/Floors.** Walls should be free of holes or water damage. Flooring should be secure and free of trip hazards.

Site Conditions

- **Falling Tower.** The house may not be within the "falling" distance of any tower or high tension electric line.
- **Flood Areas (A and V).** Flood areas require flood insurance.
- **High Noise Areas.** If average day/night noise levels are over 56 decibels, measures to reduce noise levels must be taken.
- **Abandoned Wells/Tanks.** Abandoned wells must be certified as safe and permanently abandoned, and these may be within 10 feet of home. If no certification is available, the well must be at least 300 feet from home. Underground tanks must be removed or certified as safe and properly abandoned.

Resources

The following list of resources has been provided to assist you. The contact information for each is following by a brief description of what the agency or company offers.

Reverse Mortgage Information

American Association of Retired Persons (AARP)
601 E. Street NW
Washington, D.C. 20049
1-888-687-2277
www.aarp.org/revmort

Resource for useful information on reverse mortgages and many other senior issues. Free download or call to order 1-800-209-8085 booklet: "Home Made Money: A Consumer's Guide to Reverse Mortgages."

FannieMae
3900 Wisconsin Avenue, NW
Washington, D.C. 20016-2892
www.fanniemae.com

Choose "Find a Mortgage," and then "Reverse
Mortgage." Free download or call 1-800-732-6643
to order any of the following publications:

- "Considering a Reverse Mortgage?"
- "Home Equity Conversion Mortgage
  Consumer Factsheet"
- "Home Keeper Consumer Factsheet"
- "Money From Home" (workbook)
- "Reverse Mortgage Lenders" (list)

Federal Trade Commission
Consumer Response Center
600 Pennsylvania Avenue, NW
Washington, D.C. 20580
1-877-FTC-HELP
www.ftc.gov

Website offers publications on everything from privacy to the latest scams. Free download or call
1-877-382-4357 to order brochure "Reverse
Mortgages: Proceed with Care."

Financial Freedom Senior Funding Corporation
7595 Irving Center Drive, Suite 250
Irvine, CA 92618
1-888-738-3773
www.financialfreedom.com

Offers basic information about reverse mortgages,
including Cash Account.

National Center for Home Equity Conversion (NCHEC)
360 N Robert Street, #403
St. Paul, MN 55101
(651) 222-6775
www.reverse.org

Website contains information about reverse mortgage options.

National Reverse Mortgage Lenders Association (NRMLA)
1625 Massachusetts Avenue, NW, Suite 601
Washington, D.C. 20036-2244
1-866-264-4466
www.reversemortgage.org

Website offers information, publications, and links to lender lists. Free download or call 1-866-264-4466 to order and of the following booklets:

- *The NRMLA Guide to Aging in Place*
- *Just the* FAQs, *Answers to Common Questions About Reverse Mortgages*
- *Using Reverse Mortgages for Health Care*

U.S. Department of Housing and Urban Development (HUD)
451 7th Street, NW
Washington, D.C. 20410
202-708-1112
www.hud.gov/groups/seniors.cfm

Links to housing resources and options, including approved counselors, lenders, and information about reverse mortgages.

FHA Mortgage Limits
https://entp.hud.gov/idapp/html/hicostlook.cfm

To locate HUD counselors by phone, call 1-800-569-4287.

Other State/Federal Housing Programs

Connecticut Housing Finance Authority
999 West Street
Rocky Hill, CT 06067-4005
(860) 571-3502
www.chfa.org

For information on Connecticut's Reverse Annuity Mortgage, choose the link under Elderly Programs.

Montana Department of Commerce
Housing Division
P.O. Box 200528
Helena, MT 59620-0528
1-800-761-6264
www.housing.state.mt.us

For information on Montana's Reverse Mortgage Annuity Loan program, visit the website and choose the link under Programs and Boards, Elderly Programs.

Rural Housing Service National Office
U.S. Department of Agriculture
Centralized Servicing Center
1520 Market Street
St. Louis, MO 63103
1-800-414-1226
www.rurdev.usda.gov/rhs/index.html

Information on Rural Housing Development housing programs, including Home Repair Loan and Grant Program.

U.S. Department of Energy
1000 Independence Ave., SW
Washington, D.C. 20585
www.eere.energy.gov/weatherization

Weatherization Assistance Program—Website provides information and links to state agencies for Weatherization Assistance Program. Application must be made to state agencies.

U.S. Department of Energy
1000 Independence Ave., SW
Washington, D.C. 20585
www.acf.hhs.gov/programs/liheap/states.htm

Low Income Home Energy Assistance Program (LIHEAP)—Program may provide bill payment assistance, weatherization, and energy-related repairs. Visit website or call National Energy Assistance Referral (NEAR) for more information at 1-866-674-6327.

Additional Resources

Administration on Aging
U.S. Department of Health and Human Resources
www.eldercare.gov

Eldercare Locator—Provides information on elder care alternatives for older Americans and their caregivers, as well as links to federal, state, and local assistance programs. Or call 1-800-677-1116 to speak to an information specialist.

ElderLawAnswers.com
137 Newbury Street, Floor 2
Boston, MA 02116-2912
1-866-296-5509
www.elderlawanswers.com

Website provides articles and information on Medicare, Medicaid and Social Security, estate planning, and long-term care options. Also provides links to member lawyers experienced in elder care.

FirstGov for Seniors
www.seniors.gov

FirstGov for Seniors is a gateway with direct links to all government agencies that provide services for senior citizens.

www.GovBenefits.gov

This website offers prescreening and links to government benefit sites, to help individuals find any government benefits they may qualify for.

The National Council on Aging
300 D Street, NW, Suite 801
Washington, D.C. 20024
(202) 479-1200
Main website: www.ncoa.org
www.benefitscheckup.org

Benefits CheckUp—A free service offered through
NCOA, to help seniors find resources that may
assist with some of their health care, utilities, and
housing costs. Visit the website to fill out question-
naires.

**Pharmaceutical Research and Manufacturers
of America (PhRMA)**
1100 Fifteenth Street, NW
Washington, D.C. 20005
HelpingPatients.org

Web-based program to help low-income patients
find assistance programs to obtain low-cost or free
brand-name medications. Free service includes
resources from member and nonmember companies, as well as information from federal and state
programs. Go online to fill out an application or
call for printed copy of program listings at 1-800-
762-4636.

Social Security Administration
Office of Public Inquiries
Windsor Park Building
6401 Security Blvd.
Baltimore, MD 21235
Main website: www.ssa.gov
1-800-772-1213
www.ssa.gov/notices/supplemental-security-income

Explains Supplemental Security Income (SSI), and provides links to a Benefit Eligibility Screening Tool (http://best.ssa.gov) to see if applicants qualify for this program.

Index